Fashioning a New World

A History of the
Woodcraft Folk

Fashioning a New World

A History of the Woodcraft Folk

by Mary Davis

Published to commemorate the 75th
anniversary of the Woodcraft Folk

Holyoake Books

Holyoake Books is the imprint
of the Co-operative College,
Stanford Hall, Loughborough,
Leicestershire LE12 5QR

First published December 2000

British Library Cataloguing in Publication Data

A catalogue record for this book
is available from the British Library

ISBN 0 85195 278 X

Printed in Great Britain by
Professional Book Supplies Ltd
Abingdon, Oxford

CONTENTS

ABBREVIATIONS

ADC	Annual Delegate Conference (Woodcraft Folk)
BFCY	British Federation of Co-operative Youth
BFYC	British Federation of Young Co-operators
CBCO	Central Board for Conscientious Objection
CEC	Central Education Executive (Co-operative Union)
CIMEA	Comite Internationale des Mouvements d'Enfants et d'Adolescents
CND	Campaign for Nuclear Disarmament
COs	Conscientious Objectors
Comintern	(Third) Communist International
CPGB	Communist Party of Great Britain
CWS	Co-operative Wholesale Society
CYI	Communist Youth International
CYM	Co-operative Youth Movement
FPSI	Federation of Progressive Societies and Individuals
GDR	German Democratic Republic
IFM	International Falcon Movement
IFS	International Falcon Secretariat
ILP	Independent Labour Party
IUSY	International Union of Students and Youth
NCVYS	National Council of Voluntary Youth Organisations
NCYO	National Co-operative Youth Organisation
NFC	National Folk Council
NMWM	No More War Movement
OWC	Order of Woodcraft Chivalry
RACS	Royal Arsenal Co-operative Society
SEI	Socialist Education International
SYI	Socialist Youth International
TUC	Trades Union Congress
WF	Woodcraft Folk
WFDY	World Federation of Democratic Youth
YCL	Young Communist League
YMA	Youth Movement Archive

INTRODUCTION

In 1975, Leslie Paul, the founder of the Woodcraft Folk, lamented that 50 years after its foundation no 'expert study' or 'proper history' of the Woodcraft Folk had been written. Twenty-five years on the situation has not been remedied until, I hope, now - although I cannot judge whether this is the kind of 'expert' or 'proper' book Paul had in mind. Certainly it is not the official history of the Woodcraft Folk, neither is it a celebratory monograph or a narrative history. Such a book might appeal to Folk members who would naturally search its pages for a reference to the events which they considered important or in which they were involved. However this would make dull reading for everyone else. This is not to say that an official chronicle has no place, but such tomes, worthy as they are, rarely make interesting reading for the non specialist, and often, because they are usually highly partisan, rarely make for good history.

Hence, although I was pleased to be commissioned by the Woodcraft Folk to write a history of the organisation to coincide with its 75th anniversary, I was even more pleased that those who asked me were prepared to accept my terms of reference. Whether they will be pleased with the result is another matter. However, I made it clear that it was not my aim to please anyone, but rather to attempt an historical evaluation of the Folk in its context as a very neglected part of the British Labour movement. This, it seems to me, is the real is the real point of a study of the Woodcraft Folk - not as a simple narrative in itself and for itself with all its arcane rituals and inner conflicts under the microscope, but rather as a unique youth and children's organisation, the fate of which was never solely dependent on itself, but was bound up with the fortunes of the labour movement of which it was and remains a part, and which it attempted, sometimes quirkily, but always independently, to serve.

There is hardly any secondary source material available. Although the study of youth and youth culture is, by now, an established academic sub-discipline, there is next to nothing on the relationship between the organised labour movement and youth. This is partly explained by the evident lack of interest and understanding of youth shown by the 'adult' labour movement - a fact which is illustrated by its failure to maintain its own youth wings let alone support an independent organisation. In contrast to Continental Europe, the labour and socialist movement in Britain has shown little interest in building or supporting its own organisations for children and young people. This is surprising given that its interests would be well served by providing leisure activities for the younger generation which might incline it, in later life to espouse labour movement values. Certainly the ideological purpose of winning young minds was recognised by Britain's rulers: hence the importance of the scouting movement (and similar uniformed organisations) and its rapid recognition as the acceptable recreational activity for boys.

However, despite general labour movement disinterest, a remarkable organisation was founded in 1925 as a non-militarist, pro-socialist alternative to the scouting movement. This organisation - the Woodcraft Folk - now in its 75th year, is still going strong. Many on the left of the political spectrum will have heard of it, maybe they will have participated in it when they were children or sent their own children to its camps and weekly group nights Although there were other attempts, the Woodcraft Folk is the only surviving independent youth and children's organisation with a socialist and labour movement orientation. For this reason alone a study of it is long overdue and although there are countless other reasons for investigating its past, my prime consideration as a labour historian, relates to Woodcraft's genesis and development within the labour movement.

My complete reliance on primary source material has raised important questions about archives and their enduring importance. The archive of the Woodcraft Folk (and of Kibbo Kift Kindred) is to be found in the British Library of Political and Economic Science. The archivists there are unfailingly helpful and I am greatly indebted to them. Nonetheless an archive is only as good as the material deposited in it - this depends on the organisation and its members disgorging their bounty and placing it where it can be best preserved and catalogued. The Woodcraft archive has great gaps in it - gaps which I am sure could be filled if the piles of material currently languishing in the attic of Folk House was handed over to BLEPS, and if individual members who seem to have stacks of important documents under their beds would do the same. If it were not for the fact that at least two important leaders of the Folk preserved so much of the Folk's written history AND handed it over to professional archivists, the archive would hardly exist at all. If labour movement organisations, no matter how small or obscure, do not respect their own pasts by preserving and cherishing all forms of documentation, written and oral, then they are in practice denying their history and hence their right to be remembered. There can be no objective assessment of the past without evidence. If the evidence is obscured or at worst destroyed, we will be left only with our imaginations.

I am very grateful to the staff at Folk House for their forbearance during my frequent visits. I also wish to record my thanks to the archivist and librarian at Holyoake House, the headquarters of the Co-operative Union and also to the staff at the National Museum of Labour History. Paul Bemrose has been a constant source of help and a mine of information. He is responsible for collecting an oral history archive for the Woodcraft Folk, the first fruits of which are to be seen in Appendix II of this book. I am indebted to him for permitting me to use this valuable material.

Chapter 1

YOUTH AND EMPIRE

In the last quarter of the 19th century Britain, already in possession of a large Empire, embarked in common with other major European states on a massive programme of colonial expansion. By 1914 the British Empire amounted to some 12.7 million square miles, in all five continents, with a total population of 431 million people, the overwhelming majority of whom were black.[1]

From the 1870s onwards, faced with the loss of her markets in Europe and America, Britain became increasingly reliant on her colonial empire. British colonial policy was dominated by the twin imperatives of ever tighter control of existing colonies and the relentless drive to conquer and annex new ones. She was not alone in this objective - the drive for protected markets propelled other European countries on the same course, leading to the aggressive Imperialism which characterised the period 1880-1914. This resulted in many 'small' wars between the colonisers and the colonised and heightened international tension between the colonising 'great' (and not so great powers - eg Italy, Belgium) culminating in the first world war.

Clearly such a project had huge implications for all aspects of British politics. The most obvious consequence was a massive increase in arms expenditure and personnel. Soldiers and sailors were called upon in increasingly large numbers to fight and die for the empire. However this also posed problems since such an 'active' colonial policy required, unlike in the previous half century, mass consent.

This new 'age of imperialism' was also 'the age of the masses'. By 1884 the majority of adult males had won the vote and by 1890 elementary education was free and compulsory for all. The great fear of the ruling elite was that this now literate and enfranchised working class might cast its votes against the imperialist consensus of the Tory and Liberal parties and in favour of the newly formed socialist parties (the Social Democratic Federation, 1884 and the Independent Labour Party, 1893).

It is in this context that we must view the attempts to popularise the Empire as a means of Britain's salvation during a period of relative industrial decline in the face of increasing competition from European rivals.

Imperial ideology, eugenics and racism

There was ample opportunity to disseminate the 'imperial ethic' on a mass scale given that the last quarter of the nineteenth century witnessed a great expansion, formally and informally, of the ideological apparatus of the state which was both prompted and facilitated by the rise in literacy. This was the era of the birth and the wide scale development of the popular press (dominated by the conservative magnate, Harmsworth), the propaganda poster, the music hall, the Scout movement (and other similar youth movements), the working men's club, cheaper and more popular literature (the novels of Henty and Kipling) and great national pageants like Queen Victoria's diamond Jubilee and Empire Day.

The ideology of racism had underpinned slavery and hence was not a new phenomenon. What was new, however, was that now in the era of the masses and their centrality in the imperial project, racism was transformed into a mass ideology and an ideology of the masses. Racism thus became a central feature of imperialist ideology in the late 19th century. In this period racism was dressed up in a new pseudo-scientific garb and given a populist mass appeal. School geography and history text books perpetrated racial supremacist dogma as established fact.[2] Volumes of 'scholarly' writings appeared to provide some kind of intellectual justification of British racial superiority. Hitler claimed to have been influenced by the writings of the British white supremacists of this era. He regarded their work as expressing the dominant world outlook of the British who he viewed as part of the same Anglo-Saxon 'race' to which the Germans belonged. For Hitler, therefore, the English would have been Germany's natural allies.

British 'social Darwinists' like Benjamin Kidd and Karl Pearson subverted Darwin's theory of evolution by crudely using his ideas on the 'survival of the fittest' and applying them to the struggle between races. Despite the finer points of 'theory' which divided the two men, their central concern, born out of England's declining economic position as a world power, was the question of the national 'struggle for existence', which for them was synonymous with racial superiority. *Social Evolution*, published in 1894, had established Kidd's reputation as one of the leading British sociologists of the day. He regarded marxism as the main enemy and believed that the granting of the vote to the working class and social legislation designed to improve the position of workers would damage the position of the wealthier classes and impel society in a socialist direction unless alternative mediating values replaced socialistic ones. For him these values were religion and nationalism.

Such values would inspire a devotion to the concept of duty which he counterposed to the individualism and self-seeking nature of the socialist ethic, which if left unchecked, would result in national stagnation. He asserted the superiority of the Anglo-Saxon race to which the English and the Germans belonged. This race, by virtue of its superior characteristics, had a higher 'social efficiency' which equipped it to triumph in the 'struggle for existence' on a world scale.

Karl Pearson, Professor of Applied Mathematics at University College, London did not share Kidd's antipathy to marxism. Pearson accepted much of Marx's economic teaching but his objection to socialism was the theory of class struggle and revolution. For this he substituted instead the struggle between races as the mechanism of progress. According to him the black races had already lost out in this struggle, having been conquered by the whites, hence proving the racial superiority of the conqueror. In order to prove this he created the new subject of biometrics - statistical biology. Pearson was popular among the left and was widely quoted in ILP literature and by ILP feminists like Isabella Ford.[3] Others like H G Wells and G B Shaw were similarly influenced. Pearson associated himself with the biologist Francis Galton, a cousin of Charles Darwin and Professor of 'eugenics' at London University. Galton discovered this new 'science' of eugenics, the practical application of which could, by means of selective breeding, regulate heredity and produce a super (white) race, capable of surviving the struggle for existence.

Eugenics

Almost overnight Eugenics became an established and virtually unquestioned orthodoxy. It was allied to the prevalent fear that the survival of the imperial super race was jeopardised by two problems. Firstly the decline in the birth rate, which had fallen steadily, especially among the middle class, since the 1880s and secondly the 'degenerated' condition of the masses. It is estimated that the birth rate had fallen by 21 per cent by the end of the 19th century. The medical journal *The Lancet* proclaimed that this was 'a national calamity seriously threatening the future of our race'.[4] 'Race suicide' quickly became the populist response, fuelled by alarmist articles and editorials in newspapers and magazines. Thus it was that, in a strange way Eugenics could and did appeal to the left and the right of the political spectrum.

Those on the right emphasised what might be called the negative eugenic concern: the fear of racial decline due to the preponderance of degenerated stock. They lamented the fact that it was the population of the 'rookeries and slums' with their deficient physical and mental (according to Galton) status who produced the most children.[5] Those on the left (like the Fabians) did not disagree with the assertion - indeed it was supported by many enquiries, like those of Booth (London) and Rowntree (York) but argued that more enlightened social policy could ameliorate and possibly resolve the problem. Whatever the political standpoint of its individual supporters, the Eugenics movement was united in its support for Britain's 'imperial mission'. All of them shared the view that the 'greatness' of Britain was indissolubly linked with the Empire, but that the maintenance and expansion of the colonies could only be accomplished if Britain continued to produce healthy stock. Galton summed up their views neatly: 'The nation which first subjects itself to a rational eugenic discipline is bound to inherit the earth'.[6]

Youth and empire

It is in the context of the pre-occupation with the survival of the white race in the epoch of imperialism that all the major youth movements (most of them uniformed) developed in precisely the same period as the 'new imperialism'. In fact it is argued that the very concept of adolescence, generally held to be the age between 14 and 20, was developed in this period (Gillis, Hendrick). Of particular concern was the study of working class town bred boys of post school age - they constituted the 'boy labour' problem. Between 1900-14 over 600 books and articles were published on the subject (J Davis). The Webbs argued that society's neglect of the working class boy was 'inconsistent with the maintenance of the race in a state of national efficiency'[7] and identified the problem thus:

> The gravest social symptom at the opening of the 20th century is the lack of physical vigor (sic), moral self control and technical skill of the town bred manual working boy.[8]

The rejection of 40 per cent of Boer War town bred recruits intensified concern about the deterioration of the race, especially its adolescent boys. The eugenicists used the term 'degeneracy' rather than deterioration in order to back their claim that the race itself was in peril: reform of diet and slum conditions might help ameliorate the situation, but only selective breeding would solve the underlying problem. The national stock had 'degenerated' too far for it to be able to reproduce anything but the same sickly, stunted, weak chested strain. Naturally the government (Tory administration under Balfour) was not willing to go this far - it was tantamount to admitting that the British were inferior. Nonetheless they were sufficiently alarmed, as evidenced by the establishment of the Interdepartmental Committee on Physical Deterioration in 1904. Although its report disappointed the eugenicists by rejecting the hereditary in favour of the environmental factor, the fact that it found ample evidence of 'deterioration' was enough to fuel the fire of their argument.

Thus it was that the overriding motivation behind the concerns around 'the youth question' were primarily eugenic ones, revolving around the issues of physical deterioration, and fitness for breeding. Youth according to Hendrick now had a 'new image as guardian of the race'.[9] What was needed to reverse this perceived deterioration? How were the values of duty, obedience and patriotism to be instilled into a sector of society which if left to its own devices might revert to delinquency and hooliganism? Historians of youth culture point to the end of the 19th century when 'youth' was discovered as being the period in which a distinct youth subculture developed. The establishment's antidote to this was to offer an alternative form of recreation which would be capable of inculcating the values and habits appropriate to Britain's imperial destiny. Thus it was no coincidence that a plethora of youth organisations were formed between 1883 and 1908 expressly designed to recruit working class boys. The most important ones, the Boys' Brigade (1883), the Church Lads' Brigade (1891), the Boys' Life Brigade (1899) and the Boy Scouts (1908), were all uniformed and militaristic. The ideology of all these organisations was very similar, but the methods of the Scouts differed markedly. This was because Baden-Powell was very influenced by the work of the American psychologist G S Hall[10] and his populariser and disciple, W Forbush.

Forbush wrote a layman's version of Hall's theory (*Reproducing the Race Life*), which Baden-Powell recommended his scout masters to read. (MacDonald) Hall's 'recapitulation theory' underpinned not only scouting theory and practice but much subsequent youth work, including that of the Woodcraft Folk in its early years. Hall's view was that the developmental process of a child and adolescent coincides with the stages of the development of society, from its savage to its civilised state. The adolescent, he argued, was a particularly important element in this process since it marks the transitional stage between semi and full civilisation. It is in adolescence, according to Hall that 'higher and more completely human traits are born ... the adolescent is neo-atavistic, and in him the later acquisitions of the race slowly become

15

prepotent'.[11] However the great danger was that the boundless energy of youth could be diverted into degenerate paths especially in the 'civilized' countries wherein 'perversion at every stage, and hoodlumism, juvenile crime, and secret vice seem not only increasing, but develop in earlier years' and that this trend is even more marked in urban life 'with its temptations, prematurities, sedentary occupations, and passive stimuli ... and a lessening sense for both duty and discipline'.[12]

Needless to say, whatever the merits or otherwise of Hall's psychology of childhood and adolescence, it was one which was music to the ears of eugenic imperialists. It confirmed their fears about the dangers of city life and the degeneracy of the race as well as providing a solution, which, even if it did not cure racial deterioration, would at least, by concentrating on adolescent boys, provide the prerequisites for a disciplined and dutiful army. William Forbush provided practical advice on how the adolescent boy might be tamed. He divided adolescence into 3 age groups: 12-16, 16-18, 18-24 which he said corresponded respectively to the 3 stages of adolescent development: ferment, crisis and reconstruction. The restlessness and dissatisfaction with family life which characterises these phases was, according to Forbush, associated with the formation of 'gangs'. Whereas the general perception of gang behaviour was to associate it with hooliganism, Forbush argued that society should recognise and utilise its positive aspects - 'our best part is to use the gang for all it is worth, to chaperon it unobtrusively.'[13] This was precisely what the scouts did. Baden-Powell also used many other Hall/Forbush precepts, for example, that physical activity be the basis of all work with boys; that boys and girls be organised separately on the grounds they're not interested in the same things and that 'constant intimacy between maturing boys & girls fosters an undesirable precocity and introduces unnecessarily perplexing problems.'[14] Furthermore Baden-Powell accepted Forbush's point that a youth leader should be a 'manly man' - someone boys can look up to.

Given that the aims of the scout movement were little different from other uniformed organisations for boys, the main reason for its phenomenal success over its rivals was clearly due in large measure to the methods it used - methods based on Hall's psychology of child development. The undoubted popular appeal of scouting begs, however, a much more fundamental question: why was it that, in contra-distinction to continental Europe, the mass youth organisation in Britain was anti-socialist and pro-imperialist? The answer to this is intimately connected with the fate of the socialist movement in Britain which, at this time, developed in a very different way from its European counterparts.[15] Put briefly, although trade unions were very strong in Britain, the socialist movement, which was beginning to resurrect itself in the 1880s was caught on the tidal wave of imperialist hysteria and was weakened by it. Of course, the labour movements of other European countries were affected by imperialist propaganda and practice, but in the main most of the countries of continental Europe had established independent socialist parties by the last quarter of the 19th century.

In Britain, with the exception of the Chartists in the first half of the 19th century, trade unionism took precedence over socialist politics. When, by 1900, the unions recognised at long last that they could not rely on the Liberal Party to represent their interests, the resulting political formation, the Labour Representation Committee, was a compromise between a barely established socialist tradition (the Independent Labour Party formed in 1893) and the older incorporated 'lib-labism'.[16] Although it was the main force in building the unity between the industrial and political wings of the labour movement, the Independent Labour Party paid an enormous price for its efforts. It sacrificed both its socialism and its independence for the sake of unity. The end result was a Labour Party, the ideology of which could best be described as 'labourist' rather than socialist.[17] The Party was formed solely to represent the voice of the trade unions in parliament. It did not have a constitution, nor did it admit individual members until 1918. It concerned itself purely with the parliamentary process and mobilised only to fight elections. In such circumstances it is hardly surprising that little attention was paid to such issues as 'the youth question' other than when it impacted directly on the political process or later on the function of government. Youth, like women, was a category to be aided when necessary, but not to be encouraged to think, much less act, for itself. In any case, the existing youth organisations, like the Scouts, were generally well regarded by the labour movement, the leadership of which did not challenge the underlying imperialist values. On the contrary the values of discipline and duty were regarded as being universally appropriate.

Notes

1   Peter Fryer in his *Black People in the British Empire* (Pluto, 1993) estimates that of the total population of the British Empire, only 60 million were white: less than one seventh.
2   A typical example of such racist indoctrination can be found in *A History of England*, (Fletcher and Kipling, Clarendon Press, 1911) a standard text

book, in use for many years in elementary schools. Part of the section on the West Indies reads thus:

> The prosperity of the West Indies, once our richest possession, has very largely declined since slavery was abolished in 1833. There is little market for their chief products, and yet a large population, mainly descended from slaves imported in previous centuries, or of mixed black and white races, is lazy, vicious and incapable of any serious improvement, or of work except under compulsion. In such a climate a few bananas will sustain the life of a negro quite sufficiently: why should he work to get more than this? He is quite happy and quite useless and spends any extra money he has upon finery.

3   See her *Women and Socialism*, ILP 1904
4   Quoted in R Solway *Demography and Degeneration* (1990, University of North Carolina Press), p5
5   According to Karl Pearson 40 per cent of the married population produced 70 per cent of the nation's children.
6   Quoted in Solway (op cit), p62
7   S & B Webb *Industrial Democracy*, 1920 edition (Kelly, NY, 1965), xiii
8   Op cit
9   Harry Hendrick *Images of Youth: Age, Class and the Male Youth Problem* (Clarendon Press, 1990) p96
10 1904 Hall's 'Adolescence: Its Psychology and its Relations to Physiology, Anthropology, Sociology, Sex, Crime, Religion and Education.'
11 G Stanley Hall *Adolescence* vol.1 (Appleton, NY 1904) pxiii
12 Ibid pxiv
13 W B Forbush *The Boy Problem* (6th edition Westminster Press, USA, 1907) p25
14 Ibid p61
15 For a fuller, accessible, discussion of this see Mary Davis *Comrade or Brother? The History of the British Labour Movement 1789-1951*, Pluto Press, 1993
16 'Lib-labism' was the practice developed after the Second Reform Act of 1867 whereby working class men seeking election to the House of Commons serving predominantly working class constituencies stood as Liberal candidates. The 1867 Act had extended the franchise to better paid male workers.
17 See R Miliband *Parliamentary Socialism* (Allen & Unwin 1961)

Chapter 2

ALTERNATIVES TO SCOUTING

As we have seen the period between 1883 and 1908 witnessed the growth of a uniformed male youth movement. Only the Socialist Sunday Schools founded in Battersea in 1889 existed as an alternative: although this is overstating the case since they did not become a national movement until 1909 and even then such influence as they had was confined mainly to Scotland. Nonetheless, it was the only pre-scout youth organisation which offered an alternative set of values to the tub thumping, flag waving nationalistic values of the uniformed youth movement.

Within a year of its formation the Boy Scout movement was undoubtedly the mass organisation for young males. Clearly it had found a popular formula and hence any rival organisations, while rejecting scouting's message, would have to adopt and learn from some of its methods. Thus it was that in the early 20th century, many of the alternatives to the Boy Scouts came from within scouting itself. This was not surprising given that many of these methods were not invented by Baden-Powell but were adopted and considerably adapted by him in the service of his own organisation. In fact if we are to discover the origins of the Woodcraft Folk, we must look at some of the origins of the scout movement itself.

Ernest Thompson Seton

One of the most important, although largely unacknowledged (by Baden-Powell in particular) inspirations for the scouting ideal had derived from Ernest Thompson Seton. Seton, although born in England, was raised in Canada and finally settled in the USA where, in 1902, he founded a youth organisation which he named the Woodcraft Indians. When in 1910 the Boy Scouts of America was founded, Seton merged his organisation with it and for a short time he became Chief Scout of America. Thus it was that Seton linked the notion of 'woodcraft' and 'Red Indianism' which taken together, is, to a greater or lesser degree, the common genus - despite their ideological antipathy - of both the Boy Scout and later, Woodcraft Folk organisations. The other linking ideology between the Folk and the Scouts was that of recapitulation theory. This theory argued that the developmental process of a child and adolescent coincides with the stages of the development of society, from its savage to its civilised state. Although not invented by Seton it was applied in a practical fashion to the kind of youth activities which he founded. Many of Seton's methods and much of his theory was later adopted, unacknowledged, by Baden-Powell. Seton wrote many books outlining his practical programme for 'woodcraft', a term which for him meant 'outdoor life in its broadest sense'.[1] For him the model of outdoor life was the Indian who Seton felt he had to 'defend against the calumnies of those who coveted his possessions'.[2] As in the *Birch Bark Roll*, an annual publication of Seton's which he started in 1902, his *The Book of Woodcraft* was based on 9 principles of Outdoor Life:

1   that the movement is for recreation
2   that camping is the culmination of outdoor life
3   that camps should be based on self-government with adult guidance
4   that camps must use the 'magic' of the campfire ('the focal centre of all primitive brotherhood[3])
5   that 'woodcraft pursuits' be taught since these will 'develop the finest character, the finest physique ... which, in a word *make for manhood*' (Seton's italics)[4]
6   that non-competitive tests be used in a system of 'honours by standards'
7   that there should also be 'personal decoration for personal achievements'
8   that the need for 'heroic ideal', especially for boys aged 10-15, be recognised
9   that very great importance be attached to the need for 'picturesqueness in everything'.

There were two major differences between Baden-Powell and Seton. The first was in the choice of model on which camping and outdoor life was to be based. Both recognised that such models should be found within a 'native race' which had not been softened and sullied by modern industrial life. Seton's choice was the Red Indian - a model not fully accepted by the Scouts. For Seton 'the ideal Indian stands for the highest type of primitive life. He was a master of woodcraft, and unsordid, clean, manly, heroic, self-controlled, reverent, truthful and picturesque always.'[5] He candidly admitted that this ideal type was the Indian of Fenimore Cooper and Longfellow, but nevertheless also acknowledged that white Americans treated real Indians with shocking brutality and did everything possible to justify their conquest of Native

Americans by presenting them as barbarous and blood thirsty semi-humans.

Leslie Paul, the founder of Woodcraft Folk, praised Seton's 'deadly exposure of American imperialistic treatment of the Indians'.[6] For Baden-Powell, the arch imperialist, this was going a bit too far, although he need not have worried too much. Seton's radicalism in relation to native Americans did not extend to sympathy with other oppressed peoples. According to Seton there was nothing to compare with the crimes committed against American Indians: Russian despotism wasn't nearly as bad - there was at least an excuse for it since 'Nihilists, Jews and Poles were certainly breaking the law, usually plotting against the Government, when attacked'.[7] The second - and more profound - of Seton's disagreements with the Scout movement came during the first world war. Seton opposed the war and indeed opposed the military spirit which pervaded scouting and in 1915, having quarrelled with the hierarchy, he resigned as Chief Scout of America.

It is easy to see why it was that Seton's ideas provided much of the inspiration for alternatives to the Boy Scouts. Indeed, his principle and practice of woodcraft finds many resonances, quite apart from the name itself, within the Woodcraft Folk even today. His influence can be seen in the formation of three British woodcraft movements founded between 1915 and 1925 which, (like the Boy Scouts), were different versions of Seton's movement, taking over his methods and many of his ideas, but rejecting wholly his ideals and immediate aims.[8] These were, the Order of Woodcraft Chivalry, Kibbo Kift Kindred and the Woodcraft Folk.

The Order of Woodcraft Chivalry

Kibbo Kift is remembered, not so much for its own sake, but because Woodcraft Folk emerged from it as a breakaway organisation. In terms of its lasting influence and membership[9] it was as insignificant as the Order of Woodcraft Chivalry founded by Ernest and Aubrey Westlake in 1915. Both organisations reflected a revulsion against the horrors of the first world war and shared a similar distaste for industrialisation. Both espoused internationalism and were influenced by Seton's principles. However, there the similarity ended. The Order of Woodcraft Chivalry (OWC) was co-educational and democratic. Its significance lies in the fact that it was one of the first youth organisations to include girls. Its founders, the Westlakes, were Quakers. They modified Seton's model on the grounds that, for them, the American Woodcraft Indians 'although admirable in almost all points, was obviously unadapted to English conditions'[10]. However, despite their espousal of co-education, their choice of a heroic ideal to replace the Red Indian must have been singularly unattractive to girls. The organisation was based on the chivalric ideal developed by the 'presentation of heroic knighthood' which was supposed to inspire its followers to keep 'physically fit, mentally awake and morally straight.'[11]

The emblem of the order was the shield of St George. Its slogan was 'learning by doing'. Despite this English adaptation, Seton recognised the Order as being the most authentic representation of his ideas and thus in 1923, he agreed to become its honorary Grand Chieftain. However it should be noted that the OWC was not the original invention that the Westlakes boasted. They must have been aware that a very similar organisation had been formed in the USA before the first world war by William Forbush; a leading proponent and populariser of Hall's 'reproducing race life' or recapitulation theory. This organisation, the Knights of King Arthur - an organisation for adolescent boys - was seen by Forbush as the next stage from Seton's Woodcraft Indians. The latter organisation, according to Forbush corresponded to the savage stage of childhood, whereas the Knights corresponded to the chivalric period of civilisation 'based on the romantic, hero-loving, play, constructive and imaginative instincts which ripen at about fourteen'.[12]

The purpose of the Knights of King Arthur was: 'to bring back to the world, and especially its youth, the spirit of chivalry, courtesy, deference to womanhood, recognition of the *noblesse oblige,* and christian daring, an ideal of that kingdom of knightliness which King Arthur promised he would bring back when he returns from Avalon.'[13] G Stanley Hall obviously approved of this attempt to train adolescent boys in chivalric and christian values - he was the President of the organisation. The OWC remained in existence as a very small educational organisation at least until the 1980s. Once it was formed, Woodcraft Folk, while not hostile, was somewhat dismissive of the OWC characterising it as 'bourgeois'. The charge was that it was ruled by older middle class members and 'as a result the order is more inclined to theorise about their work'.[14] Their theory was described by Paul as 'pre-war intellectual liberalism'.[15]

Kibbo Kift Kindred

Notwithstanding Ernest and Aubrey Westlake and the Order of Woodcraft Chivalry, Seton's most significant disciple in Britain was

John Hargrave, who before the first world war had risen to a prominent position in the Boy Scouts as Headquarters Commissioner for Woodcraft and Camping. With characteristic immodesty Hargrave rated his influence on the scouts very highly: 'I suppose that I had a greater direct influence upon it than anyone else, except Baden-Powell himself.'[16] Hargrave was very keen on the 'Red Indian' model (he himself was known as 'White Fox' - his adopted 'red indian' name), but although not a pacifist he fell out with the Scouts over their attitude to the first world war and before that had become 'increasingly uneasy'[17] about the future of scouting. Others shared his unease - when in 1912 the scouts were granted a Royal Charter, the military tendencies of the movement were confirmed. (Paul). Hargrave's first book on scouting, *Lonecraft*[19], published in 1913, was dedicated to Seton. As with Seton, Hargrave parted company with the Scouts on similar issues. He was invalided out of the army in 1916 (he had served as a stretcher bearer in the Dardanelles), and left the Scouts two years later. In 1920 he established his own organisation - Kibbo Kift Kindred.

In his introduction to the second edition of *Lonecraft*, (1921) John Hargrave expressed the hope that the lessons of the first world war would have been learned and that world peace and co-operation would prevail. Such a sentiment was shared by many progressives, which together with the imaginative pageantry and scout-type adventure of Kibbo Kift helps explain its, albeit limited, appeal. Nonetheless, Hargrave was at pains to point out that although Kibbo Kift was a peace movement it was not a 'peace mongers movement', that he disliked equally the word 'peace' (preferring the older word 'grith') and 'the long haired crank' associated with it.[19]

Leslie Paul described why he was attracted to the organisation:

> Hargrave ... led us into a totally new world - significantly non-European and non-Christian ... woodcraft was a way of making and providing one's manhood without becoming a soldier and dying - an ambition waning in us as the slaughter went on ... Woodcraft and Indian lore, then had this other worldly appeal in a war-torn world.[20]

Hargrave himself was, according to Paul, a magnetic personality: 'he was a typical scout 'hero'; a magical charismatic aura surrounded him.'[21]

The problem was that Hargrave was not interested for very long in running a children's/youth organisation. He set out his ambitious political agenda for Kibbo Kift early on. Four years after the Russian Revolution, an event which still entranced most sections of the left,

Hargrave clearly expressed his anti-communist vision.

> While various States and Empires are wallowing in foolish ideas of Red Revolution and Red Imperialism, it is for the Kibbo Kift to blaze a trail (however dimly) towards the Federation of Mankind.[22]

Hargrave became convinced that he himself would lead the way to the achievement of the great goal of a 'United States of the world'. He was firmly committed to the leadership principle which he thought best to have vested in one man so that 'he is allowed to lead without being hampered by the petty restrictions which are necessarily associated with committee control.'[23] This together with the name of the organisation, Kibbo Kift Kindred, which was apparently the old English for 'proof of great strength' indicated that whatever his talents, Hargrave's individualism and separatism meant that the cultish tendencies, already inherent in organisations with ungrounded ideas, assumed in Kibbo Kift alarming and unchecked proportions. In fact Kibbo Kift was, when stripped of its mystifying ritual and language, little short of the adult political fantasy of its leader, played out initially on a children's stage.

Hargrave's philosophy, despite its inconsistencies, was chilling. At its core was his desire to lead a movement of national regeneration, based on the assumption that the political, moral and economic mores of contemporary society was thoroughly degenerate, corrupt and incapable of reform. Although in the 1930s Hargrave explicitly rejected any association with fascism, his analysis of the evils of modern society and determination to build a 'League of the Strong Ones'[24] with an undisputed leader, find many echoes in the early fascist movement in Italy and Germany. In addition his emphasis on 'the splendid body ... the sound mind ... the Blazing Spirit ... the Strong Will'[25] have similar unfortunate connotations not solely confined to fascist ideology.

Until the late 1920s his perspective was set on building a youth organisation which in many respects differed little from scouting, other than the fact the Kibbo Kift included women and girls, although these were organised in a separate section. Two categories of membership were established: the Kindred and the Associates. The former was to be a 'disciplined body' wearing full uniform and equipment comprising a men's section, a women's section and the 'young kindred' (under 18s). The Associates were also divided into sections: the Green Shirt associates (a 'disciplined body' of men wearing green shirt, belt and beret); associate workers (men and women in civilian clothes but who act under Kibbo Kift discipline); associate helpers (supporters with no specific obligations).[26]

Hikes, camping and outdoor activities were regularly organised. The hikes were likely to have been strenuous if the Easter 1927 trek is anything to go by. The hikers started at 7am each day and were warned that 'laggards will be left behind'. The religious were permitted to attend church, although it is unclear how they could fit this in! Women and girls walked separately.[27]

By 1928 it was clear that youth activities were to be jettisoned in favour of a wider political mission. Hargrave himself acknowledged that Kibbo Kift 'mistook itself for a youth movement' and that 'Folk dancing and wandering around with a rucksack'[28] were not enough. In a pamphlet published in 1928, *Can the Kindred Come to Power*, Hargrave expressed the view, as suggested by the title, that the Kindred can and should become a political force capable of ruling the country. To achieve this the Kindred had to transform itself into 'a well ordered and highly disciplined body' in which 'democratic talk' was replaced by 'strict training. No slop. No Chat'[29]. Opposition to such a strategy would not be tolerated. The Kindred would be 'winnowed' - Hargrave would not tolerate internal bickering and 'pseudo-psychoanalytical outpourings' - he was 'determined not to be defeated by a swamp of emotional splurge ... you cannot have individual freedom to express personality ... given the great work to be done.'[30] In his unpublished autobiography, Hargrave, reflecting on the same period, expressed the same anti-democratic sentiments, even more forcefully:

> We had to strengthen our membership against the intellectualised gabble of glib-tongued phrasemongers whose minds were sodden with the shibboleths of democracy.[31]

The accomplishment of Hargrave's 'great work' posed a major problem - Kibbo Kift was a tiny and unknown sect. Hargrave overcame this difficulty, like all anti-democrats, by asserting that political power is not dependent on the ballot box. He acknowledged, however, that no group can take power without a 'mandate of the people', but claimed that this can be manifested through the 'popular will' (which he defined as unarmed mass pressure). Bypassing parliament and the electoral process in this way was, according to Hargrave, entirely justified because the political system had reached a terminal state of decay, especially in the conditions prevailing after the General Strike of 1926 which, in his view, were further proof of administrative confusion and internal crisis. Again the parallels with fascism are strikingly obvious: the strong leader and elite group willing to take advantage of chaos by staging a coup. Of course, the similarity is purely theoretical given that the economic and political situation in Britain hardly matched that of Italy in 1922 or Germany in 1933. Hargrave regarded both sides in the conflict of 1926 as wrong - A J Cook (the miners' leader) and Winston Churchill were, he asserted as bad as each other. By 1929 Hargrave had abandoned all pretence at a youth organisation and jettisoned the exotic green jerkins and mystical symbolism of Kibbo Kift in favour of a more military style green uniform in the service of 'social credit'. This was a movement founded by Major C H Douglas which argued that the country's economic ills were the result of the money supply being controlled by the banking system rather than being based on the real wealth of the nation - its goods, plant and machinery.[32]

How was it that the Woodcraft Folk, an undoubtedly progressive labour movement organisation, emerged from such unpromising beginnings? Despite the shortcomings of Kibbo Kift and the dubious nature of its philosophy, it was among a number of organisations formed after 1918 which reflected the steadily fermenting abhorrence of war and the militaristic national chauvinism which had resulted in the disastrous world war of 1914-18. This mood went together with a rejection of the values of industrial society and the unhealthiness of town life. It expressed itself in an unformulated and idealistic desire to build something new from the ashes of a decayed civilization. Leslie Paul was one of the young men searching for an alternative vision. For him Kibbo Kift 'was like a new wind blowing through our young country ... we were certain that we were the new elite, and that by some mystical process we had been chosen to transform the world'[33].

The 'back to nature' ideal of the simple life and physical fitness, unencumbered by the patriotic agenda captured the imagination and helps explain why Kibbo Kift, at first, attracted the support of a number of well-known progressives like H G Wells, the Pethick-Lawrences[34] (leading figures in the movement for women's suffrage), Norman Angell (author of *The Great Illusion*) and many others including the Royal Arsenal Co-operative Society. So if Kibbo Kift captured the national mood and was supported by some famous names, why didn't it become a mass organisation instead of remaining a cranky and tiny sect?[35] Clearly some of the explanation is to be found in the style of Hargrave's leadership, which in 1924 had become so intolerable that many of its supporters withdrew. This included the Royal Arsenal Co-operative Society (RACS). According to Joseph Reeves, the education secretary of the RACS, his organisation was speedily disillusioned with Hargrave and was forced to withdraw when, 'we ... found that Kibbo Kift was not the type of organisation for junior co-operators'.[36]

H G Wells

Another explanation for Kibbo Kift's failure is that it was founded upon shaky theory. This theory was not invented by Hargrave, although he adapted it for his own purposes. It was a unique English creation - a form of left wing positivism which was anti marxist and anti democratic. Its leading exponent in was H G Wells who signed the Kibbo Kift covenant very early on. Today Wells is known as a novelist, but in the period between the wars he exercised considerable intellectual and political influence. During his lifetime he wrote 110 books and 500 articles. Many of the books were novels, but they all had a 'message' of one sort or another. He also wrote non-fiction, the most important of which was his two volume *Outline History of the World*. He was persuaded of the overriding importance of the power of ideas in history and hence took a strong interest in education and educational experiment of which Kibbo Kift appeared to be a promising example. For Wells the first world war was a product of men's folly - it was indicative of a defective education. Ergo, for the world to be saved, a new world order had to be created and this could only be accomplished if men's minds had been trained in a purposeful way.[37] His writings are peppered with variously expressed notions of the need for world revolution to be achieved by a super educated, intelligent elite cadre force in what he termed 'the open conspiracy'. This was a vision which clearly inspired Hargrave. Indeed Leslie Paul, also an admirer of Wells, argued that Kibbo Kift's aim since 1925 was to fulfil H G Wells' vision. Wells was not the only thinker whose dissatisfaction with society and impatience for social change led to the advocacy of anti-democratic solutions, but he was one of the most persuasive and well known of the genre.

Of more importance is the fact that the scout movement, already very strong, was adept enough to perceive the change in the national mood, and itself began to shift, albeit in an anti-communist way, in a pro-League of Nations, pro-brotherhood of man direction.[38] Although, as Leslie Paul noted, this shift in the tenor of scouting was purely expedient. Scouting's very success in exporting the movement to other countries made it difficult to reconcile their 'primitive nationalism' with claims of 'international brotherhood' and that in reality 'it has tempered its pre war militarism without, however, radically revising its views'.[39] Hence, in practice, the scouting movement remained as patriotic and imperialist as when first started. Nonetheless, it may well be that the

27

rivals to scouting underestimated the extent to which scouting could capture this new peace-loving terrain. Certainly Baden-Powell put across a very different message in 1929 compared to that of 20 years previously. The 1929 International Scout Jamboree at Birkenhead was enormous, with contingents from 42 different countries. At it Baden-Powell proclaimed:

> We alone have the universal ear of the young. Let us set about teaching that the highest virtues are friendliness and goodwill. And there will be no more war.[40]

Perhaps the most obvious explanation for the failure of Kibbo Kift and the Order of Woodcraft Chivalry lies in the fact that, paradoxically, they were too similar to the scout movement. It would be going too far to say that scouting ultimately adopted the values of the rebel breakaway groups, but given the paucity of the latter's resources and the fact that their own ideologies were so muddle-headed, they failed to take full advantage of the only really distinguishing feature of their existence, namely their internationalism and pacifism. In all other respects their activities and the theory on which such activity was founded - recapitulation theory - was very similar to the scout movement. Hence, unlike continental Europe, the British left failed to capitalise on the brief moment in the inter war period when the pacifist and internationalist message engaged with a wider audience. This was the time when it may have proved possible to build a mass based alternative youth movement. Those who were in the position to do so failed dismally to meet this challenge.

Notes

1   Ernest Thompson Seton *The Book of Woodcraft and Indian Lore*, Constable 1927, pv
2   Ibid
3   Ibid p5
4   Ibid
5   Ibid p8
6   L Paul *The Early Days*, Woodcraft Folk 1980, p2
7   Ibid p17
8   Brian Morris 'Ernest Thompson Seton and the Origins of the Woodcraft Movement', Journal of Contemporary History, vol.5 no.2 1970
9   I O Evans estimated that by 1930 OWC had 500 members and KKK 200
10 Aubrey T Westlake *Woodcraft Chivalry*, Order of Woodcraft Chivalry, 1917 p5

11 Ibid p2
12 W B Forbush *The Boy Problem* (6th edition, Westminster Press, USA, 1907), p100
13 Ibid p101
14 Anon article (probably L Paul) in *The Herald of the Folk*, February 1931 YMA.WF.331
15 *Herald of the Folk* July 1930. This comment was contained in a review of I O Evans' book *Woodcraft and World Citizenship* of which Paul was critical on the grounds that it was too partisan (Evans having been a member of KKK) and illustrative of Evans 'lack of social sense'. (This was presumably a less direct way of Paul saying that Evans was not a socialist.)
16 John Hargrave's unpublished autobiography *They Can't Kill the Sun* YMA.KK.214
17 Ibid
18 J Hargrave *Lonecraft: the Official Handbook of the Lonecraft Boys of the Woodcraft Kindred*, Constable, 1921
19 J Hargrave *The Kibbo Kift: its Aims and Methods*, New Cambridge, June 4th 1927
20 *Early Days* op cit p2
21 L Paul *Angry Young Man*, p54, Faber 1951
22 Foreword to *Lonecraft* (1921 edn) p4
23 J Hargrave *What is the Kibbo Kift* undated leaflet YMA/KKK/70-2
24 Ibid. Hargrave suggests that this is an alternative translation of 'Kibbo Kift'
25 J Hargrave *The Kibbo Kift: Its Aims and Methods*, reproduced in *The New Cambridge* June 4th 1927
26 Leaflet *The Kibbo Kift* nd YMA/KKK/70-2
27 KKK circular: Spring Festival 1927, ibid
28 J Hargrave *The Kindred*, leaflet, nd, ibid
29 Ibid
30 J Hargrave *The Winnowing of the Kin*, handwritten leaflet, 1928, ibid
31 *They Can't Kill the Sun*, nd KKK/YMA/214
32 For a fuller account of social credit see J L Finlay *John Hargrave, the Green Shirts and Social Credit* in Journal of Contemporary History, vol.5 no.1 1970
33 L Paul *Angry Young Man* p54
34 In fact Kibbo Kift was founded in the Pethick-Lawrences' house in Lincoln's Inn, London
35 In 1924, its peak year, the total attendance at the annual camp was 236
36 Joseph Reeves *Sixty Years of Stupendous Progress* 1938 (pamphlet commemorating the Diamond Jubilee of the RACS) YMA/WF/126
37 For a more thorough account of Wells' philosophy see W Warren Wagar *H G Wells and the World State*, Yale University Press, 1961
38 This argument is well made by Paul Wilkinson *English Youth Movements, 1908-30*, 'Journal of Contemporary History', vol.4, no.2, 1969
39 L Paul *The Republic of Children* (George Allen & Unwin, 1938), p21

Chapter 3

FORMATION AND EARLY YEARS

Dissatisfaction with the direction of Kibbo Kift Kindred and anger with the autocratic leadership of John Hargrave was a direct cause of the split within the Kibbo Kift from which Woodcraft Folk emerged. The Kindred archive contains an undated document with the self explanatory albeit cumbersome title 'that the administration of the Kibbo Kift during recent months has been profoundly unsatisfactory'.[1] This was presented as a motion, debated at the Althing (or annual general meeting) of 1924 and was signed by 32 members including Leslie Paul. It expressed the simmering discontent of the rebels encapsulated in a series of criticisms directed against Hargrave's leadership. The motion drew particular attention to the way in which Hargrave as Headman (leader) eliminated potential and actual opposition to his command. For example Hargrave 'blackspotted' (expelled) members without due process,[2] that under the Headman's instructions all applicants for membership were issued with a list of 25 'impertinent' questions enquiring into their religious and political beliefs[3] and that members (kinsfolk) were disenfranchised for not wearing correct costume. In addition Hargrave was criticised for his hostile attitude to the Boy Scouts and for constantly presenting his own views as that of the Kindred.

In view of Hargrave's openly stated dictatorial views, the only surprising thing about the 1924 revolt is that it did not come sooner. It was sparked by a particular event in which Leslie Paul, unwittingly, played a major part. Hargrave had refused to give formal recognition to a group in south east London (Brokleything) comprising of members in Camberwell, Deptford and Lewisham, on the grounds that their elected Headman, Leslie Paul (Little Otter), was under age - he was then 17. In his autobiography[4], Paul acknowledged the role he played in bringing together the scattered members in south east London, but says that the real leader was Gordon Ellis and that he, Paul, 'was no more than a mere figurehead'. This refusal to recognise the south east London group clearly undermined local democracy within the Kin and, taken together with all the other issues, led to the withdrawal of the rebels who comprised around a third of the membership of the Kibbo Kift.

So far this amounted to no more than a squabble within an obscure organisation and might have ended as a historical footnote in the dismal tale of Kibbo Kift, were it not for two important factors. One is that the small rebel group had the support of the Royal Arsenal Co-operative Society in the form of its education secretary, Joseph Reeves. This fact was clearly acknowledged by Paul in one of the first documents presented for approval of Folk Council.[5] In it Paul states the following:

> The Woodcraft Folk Movement, having its birth in the Royal Arsenal Co-operative Society, under the leadership and inspiration of young people may be properly described as the first youth movement, within Co-operative spheres, that gives coherent and conscious expression to the ideals and philosophy of young people ... and constitutes a break away from the old tradition of study circles and recreational groups.

The other factor was that the rebels had a distinctive socialist ideology which had the potential to attract labour movement support.[6] As Paul notes, without the support of the working class and labour movement 'Hargrave had forfeited for ever the chance of building his movement into a powerful and independent Left Scout Movement',[7] assuming of course that such a project was ever Hargrave's aim in the first place. As we have seen, such an assumption was erroneous and valuable time had been wasted in the Kindred by those who genuinely held such a vision. The split in Kibbo Kift did not result in the formation of a new organisation, the Woodcraft Folk, until a year later, and even then its beginnings were so unpromising that it hardly seemed destined to last 75 days, much less 75 years.

Leslie Paul

Leslie Paul together with his friend Sidney Shaw started a small group in Lewisham in February 1925, the Wayfarers' Fellowship, consisting of four small boys, later joined by some girls who were all recruited from the Co-operative Junior Guild which met at Holbeach Road School. With a total membership of 70 by December 1925, mainly concentrated in the south London area, it took a leap of faith to believe that the grandly titled Federation of Co-operative Woodcraft Fellowships could aspire to becoming a children's and youth organisation of any national significance. Six or seven new groups were started following the formation of the Mossbank Lodge. This was the result of a meeting of 20 or so of Paul's friends in the back garden of his home in Forest Hill. One of the first decisions of the newly established Folk Council was, on Paul's suggestion, to adopt three strategic tasks. The first was the one accorded the greatest importance; this was to organise children's groups with a definite educational programme. The second was to rally co-operative youth to woodcraft ideals and the third was to rally support for the new organisation in the co-operative and socialist movement.[8]

Of course, all three tasks should have been inter-related, but it is clear that because the first was prioritised and the organisation was so small, inadequate attention was paid to the others in the early years. A great deal of effort was spent in working out the educational programme and activities of the Folk. However, even though Shaw and Paul were socialists, there seemed little, at first, to distinguish their efforts from Kibbo Kift. Paul's admiration for Ernest Tompson Seton was evident in the choice of the name 'Woodcraft Folk'. The word 'woodcraft' showed the connection of the new organisation with Seton's theory and practice, while the term 'folk' showed the influence of the Germanic youth movements. As Paul explained,[9] the word was used in the sense of 'volk' (people) and not in the 'arty-crafty' sense. 'Tribal training' was central to the activity of the fledgling movement. Paul described how, in 1926, he attended a meeting organised by the Order of Woodcraft Chivalry, at which Seton was the main speaker.[10] After the meeting Seton practised 'Red Indian' dancing with his audience, beating rhythms out on his 'tom-tom'. This inspired Paul to write his own dances for the Woodcraft Folk, thus cementing what is often regarded as the Folk's peculiar attachment to 'red indianism' as a form of 'tribal training'.[11] Like other youth leaders of his day, Paul's ideas were based on recapitulation theory, the theory upon which 'tribal training' was predicated. For Paul the value of recapitulation theory was that it recognised that a child's changing 'desires and demands and powers of expression vary considerably from epoch to epoch - from year to year'.[12] Hence the division of the Folk into age groupings with appropriate activities for each. In his oral testimony (see Appendix II), Paul claimed that he gradually abandoned the theory, but this is not to say that it was abandoned by the Folk.

The 'articles of faith' Paul proclaimed in *The Folk Trail*[13] were little different from Seton's Woodcraft Indians or that of Kibbo Kift. Indeed many of them would have been familiar to the Boy Scouts. Paul argued that camp life and open-air events like hiking had to be an essential part of youth activity in order to provide a healthy environment as an antidote to the evils of industrialism. Camping was also important because it provided an education in the day-to-day practicalities of co-operative living and shared social endeavour. As with Kibbo Kift, one finds in the early Woodcraft Folk a sustained attack on commercialism, industrialism and the 'crushing of individuality in the schools'. The Folk, especially its camping and outdoor activities, was thus seen as 'rescue work' insofar as it 'lifts young people out of the apathy of civilization'. All such activity was to be based on 'tribal life' since this 'presents the boy with a form of organisation he can understand and enjoy. The simple government of the gang invites his participation and the ideal of service to his fellows is first learnt ... in the realisation of his duty to the gang'.[14] (Despite constant references to boys in its early literature, the Woodcraft Folk was, nonetheless co-educational from the outset). Pageantry ceremony & song was, Paul argued, a vital element in retaining a child's interest, but was also important because it provided active recreation rather than passive amusement. Finally, he asserted that the teaching of world history and evolution was essential to ensure that the boy enriches his mind with 'the correct historical "perspective"'[15] so that 'we may understand and revere the Great Spirit' The 'Great Spirit'[16] was another American Indian conception which was used in order to acknowledge that 'man does not live by bread alone but is a creature of music, art, dancing and poetry from whom a touch of 'cosmic piety' is appropriate.'[17]

Underlying all Folk activity was an educational philosophy, based on an adaptation of the 'learning by doing' ideas of Jean-Jacques Rousseau and Herbert Read, which was intended to give meaning to the otherwise arcane woodcraft practices. In the case of the Folk it would seem that the theory was grafted on to practices already inherited.

> Our education is not a matter of little moral talks or stilted lectures, it is a system where the primal instincts of the child are moulded along a social path by the very things a child loves ... our principles of training permeate the whole of our activities; every symbol, every totem, every song has its own peculiar value ... we feel that it is necessary, if the race is to survive, to produce men and women who by their knowledge, their physical fitness and their mental independence shall bring quick sure brains and boundless vitality to bear on man's struggle for liberty. We are the revolution ... we are paving the way for that re-organisation of the economic system which will mark the re-birth of the human race.

During his own lifetime Paul re-interpreted these, his own words, in different ways. In his autobiography, although retaining some sympathy for the notion of 'learning by doing', he condemned the overall 'philosophy' as 'new paganism ... and a new barbarism'[19] because it rejected all ideas other than those implicit in the woodcraft way which he castigated as 'window dressing, unconsciously indulged in to satisfy the prevailing 'left' climate of those years'.[20] Years later, Paul presented a more benign view of the early educational theory of the Woodcraft Folk. He wrote that despite the use of the phrase 'we are the revolution', the Folk did not base itself on the notion of an economic revolution:

> What it was seeking was a new way of living, a richer day-to-day life in the present, in fact a cultural revolution.[21]

The social aims of the new organisation, as stated in its Charter, displayed an eclectic brew which could have appealed to racial supremacists, eugenicists, progressives, socialists and cranks at the same time:

> We feel that it is necessary, if the race is to survive, to produce men and women who by their knowledge, their physical fitness and their mental independence shall bring quick, sure brains and boundless vitality to bear on man's struggle for liberty. We are the revolution. With the health that is ours and with the intellect and physique that will be the heritage of those we train we are paving the way for that reorganisation of the economic system which will mark the rebirth of the human race.[22]

Paul acknowledged that initially he was profoundly influenced by eugenics, albeit of a left wing variety. His analysis of the failure of the General Strike was a eugenic one. He asserted that 'you can't get A1 socialism from C3 people' - new and better human material was required to rebuild the wreckage left by capitalism. Indeed this was one of the chief arguments for the need for an organisation like Woodcraft Folk.

However, despite the similarities with other organisations, and the somewhat dubious and badly formulated nature of some of its ideas, the Woodcraft Folk was different. The essential differences between the Folk and its predecessors was the fact that the Folk was a democratic and egalitarian organisation, genuinely co-educational, based on the working class and motivated by a socialist vision of the future. In other words, all its activities were directed towards a very different purpose from that of any other children's or youth organisation. Paul and his generation were much influenced by William Morris's brand of socialism which combined an idealised vision of aspects of the past with a poetic vision of a socialist future. Morris was an artist, designer writer and poet as well as being a founder of the Socialist League and editor of its journal *Commonweal*. Paul loved Morris's poetry and many lines of it appear in Woodcraft Folk literature. The following passage, often quoted by Paul and attributed to Morris is now the Woodcraft Folk 'Creed' - it is recited by all children and adults at the beginning of all group meetings and at daily at camps:

> This shall be for a bond between us
> That we are of one blood you and I,
> That we have cried peace to all
> And claimed kinship with every living thing,
> That we hate war sloth and greed
> And love fellowship,
> And that we shall go singing to the fashioning
> Of a new world.

Undoubtedly many were attracted to the Folk by the outdoor life and the colourful pageantry, but others like Joseph Reeves saw the Folk's potential as 'the militant part of the co-operative youth movement'.[23] Certainly the first formal document adopted by the governing body of the new organisation, the Folk Council, must have satisfied those, who, like Joseph Reeves, backed the Folk. It declared that Woodcraft Folk was 'the first movement within Co-operative spheres, that gives coherent and conscious expression to the ideals and the philosophy of young people'. Its philosophy was defined as:

> healthy living, hard thinking and obedience to the evolution of the human race. It preaches the development of the individual that he may serve the race better, the rebirth of the communal life of the people that we may steer clear of the dogmas of capitalism ... to transform the economic system to one of economic freedom for the worker and communal control of the means of production.

G S M Ellis, an active co-operator, predicted that the Woodcraft Folk would succeed because it would not make the same mistake as its predecessors since unlike them 'it put socialist reorganisation at the front' of its programme and because it 'recognised that there must be fundamental economic changes before the philosophy of well living will be established universally.'[24]

Thus in terms of the priority it had set itself, Woodcraft Folk, within its first four years of existence had indeed set out its educational policy, aims and programme, albeit much of it was to evolve in a more coherent direction over the next few years. But what of the other two tasks the Folk had agreed at the first meeting of its Folk Council - to rally co-operative youth to its ideals and to rally support for the new organisation in the co-operative and socialist movement? Here its success was more limited due to two factors. The first is that the Folk made the mistake in the early years (rectified in the 1930s), of remaining aloof from the labour movement and its activities. Hence apart from its link with the RACS and the evident goodwill shown towards it by many co-operators, it was virtually unknown in other circles. Despite good intentions it still inhabited the rather closed world of a social experiment orchestrated untiringly by Leslie Paul and a group of close associates. This was partly the inevitable result of daring to try something different, but it was also a consequence of the fact that at this stage, the Folk had not fully broken with the sectarian past from which it had emerged, although it had the potential so to do. But there was also another, perhaps more objective reason connected with the then state of the labour movement. Clearly this was a factor outside the control of the Folk.

The terrain for the labour movement and socialist ideas generally was much less favourable in the late 1920s than it had been immediately after the war. In particular, the defeat of the General Strike in 1926, a year after the formation of Woodcraft Folk, which gave rise to a mood of pessimism among socialists in the labour movement, did not augur well for the development of the new organisation. Leslie Paul, who was very involved in supporting the strike, acknowledged the impact of its defeat.

> Tragically so very soon after our foundation the Labour Movement lost its impulse to expansion and experiment. The 1926 General Strike produced a sad apathy among socialists and co-operators.

During the strike, councils of action were set up in most localities. Paul was on the executive of the one established in Lewisham. In common with most activists, he regarded the TUC's decision to call off the strike after 9 days as a 'great betrayal' and hence threw himself into youth work with greater vigour. For a while he despaired of the labour movement and he saw Woodcraft Folk as an escape:

We found that the working-class movement was itself stuffy and middle-class and its endless trade-union meetings in pubs, and smoky political meetings in drab halls, boring and useless when one might be out in the countryside.[26]

The co-operative movement was similarly criticised. The Folk, it was claimed, would appeal to 'those who feel that the co-operative movement gains nothing by being as stuffy and as colourless as a puritan meeting' - a sentiment hardly calculated to nurture the hand that fed it!

These two factors - the way in which the Woodcraft Folk developed and the atmosphere in which this development proceeded - have to be taken together to get a convincing explanation as to why it did not make more of an impact within the labour movement in the early years.

The first four years of the Folk's existence (again according to Paul) were spent in laying the foundations of the Folk and planning future development. After 1929 the Folk recognised in a much clearer way than it did in the first four years that its 'place was in the general working class movement'[27] and as a result of this and its consequent involvement in anti-fascist activities in the 1930s (see chapter 6), Paul and others advocated a break with some of the more arcane rituals of the Kibbo Kift past. However, the only tangible result of Paul's proposals for 'A New Scheme of Folk Government' drawn up in 1934 was to abolish the Althing (annual meeting of members) and institute instead a National Delegate Conference. When Paul resigned as Headman in 1934 it was clear that an era in Folk history had ended. That is not to say that there was any major policy shift - the Folk, under Paul's leadership had already been set on a socialist course and was immersed in the peace and anti-fascist fight. It was clear, however, that more fundamental change was required if it was to fulfil its potential and become a much larger organisation.

The fact that the RACS recognised and financially supported the new organisation was remarkable and very far sighted. However, by 1935 it was evident that even this, the Folk's most staunch supporter, thought that change was necessary. An article[28] by Joseph Reeves questioned the usefulness of some of the Folk's ways and wanted the Folk to consider whether it was 'concerned more with forms of organisation than with social emancipation?' He explained:

> Is the dress we wear more important than the great drive towards the ideal of self government? Is the clinging to Indian

names keeping out the self conscious and rather fastidious young person? Are we willing to compromise on these unimportant things so as to be the vehicle of the uprising of the new generation towards vastly changed standards of life?

Like Paul, Reeves suggested that a simplified form of Folk costume was necessary and that more modern ceremonies should be introduced. No-one, he argued, in the 'general public' could possibly understand the Folk's use of the 'totem and tom-tom .... These appear to be reversions to savagery'. It was, he said, vitally important to accept the age we live in - there could be no going back to any idealised past and 'in entering into this new world, it is important that we should not be encumbered by a tradition which will hamper us in our work of bringing it about.' When Gordon Ellis first told Reeves about Woodcraft Folk, the former described it as 'the cult of the free' and thus, Reeves warned 'it would be a terrible thing if such a movement found its style being cramped by a cast-iron tradition which denied it its own freedom.'

Although many of 'these cast iron traditions' did not change until after the second world war, the Folk itself had changed by the 1930s. It had become a left wing youth organisation with a distinctly socialist orientation. Although Paul and others continued to insist upon the importance of child training, he also frequently referred to the Folk as a youth movement, 'not in the narrow sense' since it was open to all, including, of course, adults who signed its Charter. It was for this reason that the Althing of 1933 received a 'youth activity report' in which discussion was invited on the desirability of establishing a separate youth section within the Folk. In addition members were asked to consider how the peace and anti-imperialist message of the Folk 'and its co-operative and socialist doctrine' can be best imparted to pioneers. The result of the debate was the formation of 'Hardihood Lodges' for the over 16s. There was a fine balance to be struck, especially in the politically charged atmosphere of the 1930s between, the needs of the different categories of the membership of the Folk - children, youth and adults. With the experience of Kibbo Kift in mind, this was clearly a problem which Paul recognised. In his view a healthy test for a children's/youth movement was whether it existed to ensure survival of the adult organisation or whether it was genuinely based on the needs of the young. He wrote:

It is bad for the child - and bad for the grown ups - if the organisation that brings them together exists only for the purpose of imposing a fixed set of ideas on the mind of the child.[29]

Ironically, it was in the 1930s, when the Folk was at its most political, that it began to grow from under a thousand members in 1930 to over 5,000 by 1939. However, unlike Kibbo Kift, its politics were not dogmatic or sectarian and nether did it neglect its primary purpose was as a children's organisation. When, in 1934, Paul resigned for health reasons as Headman, he could, had he chosen, take some pride that the organisation he had founded was soundly based and was beginning to be noticed within the labour movement.

Paul's own journey, however, following his detachment from Folk activism, was to take him far away from socialist ideology in general and the Folk in particular. He rejected marxism in favour of religion and sought to distance himself from the activities of his youth and early manhood. In 1951 he wrote:

> Leftism now seemed to me to be some kind of disease itself, which I had caught when young, and never became cured of, a disease like that strange condition in which a man loses his sense of balance and crawls and swarms over the earth in the most nauseating contortions when what he most needs is to walk upright.[30]

Nonetheless, Woodcraft Folk, the movement Paul founded, did not share his disillusion. It continued to be inspired by socialist ideas, even though the way this has been expressed throughout its history has changed markedly.

As the interview with Paul (see appendix II) shows, he regarded the Woodcraft Folk much more fondly in the years before his death. The views he expressed in the 1970s bore little resemblance to the bitter cathartic outpourings of his autobiography.

Notes

1   YMA/KK/2
2   This was a particular reference to Eric C Peake (alias Wanderwolf) of Epping.
3   This is presumably a reference to the section on applicants in a leaflet (undated) entitled *What is the Kibbo Kift?* ,YMA/KK/70-2
4   L Paul, *Angry Young Man*, 1951 p59
5   *Little Otter's Memorandum to the Folk Council*, February 6th 1926. 'Little Otter' was Leslie Paul's Folk name. I found this rare original document,

annotated by Leslie Paul, by chance whilst looking for something else in the WF archive in Folk House.

6   Leslie Paul dated his own 'initiation' into socialism from the 1923 General Election where as an assistant agent in the Tottenham constituency he met many prominent Labour Party figures including Ramsay Macdonald, Hugh Dalton, Harold Laski, the Pethick-Lawrences, George Lansbury and others.

7   Ibid

8   *Little Otter's Memorandum to the Folk Council*, February 6th 1926

9   For example in *Angry Young Man*, op cit

10 L Paul *Early Days of the Woodcraft Folk*, WF 1975

11 Until 2000, the 'red indianism' of the Folk was apparent at every gathering. The form of greeting and assent was the word 'How'. At every camp the children would erect tepees. Part of the chorus to the frequently sung *Who Are These Folk* is as follows:
        Hark the beating of our tom-tom
        See the fire before our wig-wam ...
    The Annual Delegate Conference of 2000 resolved to break with the 'red indian' tradition.

12 *The Folk Trail* p21

13 Ibid p22

14 *The Folk Trail* p22

15 Ibid p23

16 WF Charter

17 *Early Days*, p9, op cit

18 From L Paul *Child and the Race*, quoted in L Paul, *Angry Young Man*, op cit, p63

19 *Angry Young Man*, p62

20 Ibid p64

21 L Paul *The Early Days of the Woodcraft Folk*, WF 1980 pp10-11

22 Quoted in L Paul ibid p63

23 JReeves 'The Co-operative Movement and Woodcraft Folk', *The Helper*, vol.1 no.1, March 1927, YMA/WF/31

24 'An open Letter to Little Otter' signed Shada (G S M Ellis). This letter congratulating Leslie Paul (Little Otter) on his election as WF Headman was not made public until Paul retired in 1934. It is undated but must be 1925. YMA/WF/6

25 'Message from the retiring Headman to the Althing' 1934, YMA/WF/6

26 *Angry Young Man*, p62

27 Message from retiring Headman (L Paul) to 1934 Althing, YMA/WF/6

28 J Reeves 'Away with Tradition', *The Helper*, vol II no 11 June 1935 pp7-8, WF archive

29 *The Folk Trail*, p16

30 *Angry Young Man*, p296

Chapter 4

THE CO-OPERATIVE MOVEMENT

As a previous chapter has indicated, the Royal Arsenal Co-operative Society (RACS) was closely connected with Woodcraft Folk from the outset. However, the attitude of the RACS did not typify that of the umbrella body: the Co-operative Union. It was not until 1927 that the Woodcraft Folk gained recognition at a national level. In that year the Central Education Committee (CEC) of the Co-operative Union agreed to give the Folk a small grant and in 1929 the CEC, after a meeting with Leslie Paul and Joseph Reeves, agreed that the co-operative movement should be encouraged to establish Woodcraft Folk groups and that the publications department of the Co-operative Union should include *The Folk Trail* in their list. Thus, it would appear, the scene was set for a close and harmonious relationship between the two organisations of the kind that exists today.

However, this was not the case. Although the Woodcraft Folk always regarded itself as a co-operative organisation in the broadest sense of the word, it jealously guarded its own autonomy - a fact, which more than any other, led to a stormy and sometimes hostile relationship with the Co-operative Union. At a national level, Co-op/Woodcraft Folk relations were far from good during the 1930s and 1940s. They were almost non-existent from 1946 to 1958. Frustration with the parsimony and controlling nature of the Co-operative Union in the pre-1946 period aroused the frequently expressed anger and impatience of Leslie Paul. Paul, as Woodcraft Folk Headman, was central to all the negotiations with the Co-operative Union and was highly critical of the outcome. Writing in his autobiography in 1951, he offered the following reflection:

> ... today I regret nothing more than the time I spent trying to evoke some generosity towards the Folk from the officials of the vast and unworkable co-operative bureaucracy .... The really unforgivable thing to them was that Paul had gone and built up a movement without asking their permission first.[1]

Co-operative Youth

Whilst this comment must be taken in the context of Paul's disillusionment with the labour movement (a sentiment which colours

41

his autobiography throughout), an examination of the evidence shows that his judgement was not wide of the mark.

The RACS and its education committee remained supportive of the Folk throughout its entire history, as did some other co-operative societies, but such support was never strong enough to win a permanent majority on the national body - the Central Education Committee of the Co-operative Union. The national body placed its resources at the disposal of its own youth organisations - that is to say, ones which it had created itself and which were answerable to the parent body. Clearly the Folk did not fall into this category. At almost the same time that Woodcraft Folk was founded the Co-operative Union established its own nationally co-ordinated youth wing in 1924, the British Federation of Co-operative Youth (BFCY). This developed from the Youth Circles which had been established in many regions before the first world war. These Youth Circles, later named Comrades' Circles were intended to cater for the 15-25 age group[2] and hence appeared not to compete with the Folk which appealed to a younger age group. Nonetheless, the short history of Comrades' Circles from their inception in 1922 to their closure in 1937, seems to vindicate the Woodcraft Folk's insistence on autonomy. The same lesson could be learned from the fate of the BFCY and its successors, the British Federation of Young Co-operators (BFYC) and the Co-operative Youth Movement (CYM). All three organisations were created and destroyed by the Co-operative Union.

During the 1930s Joseph Reeves was a member of the Co-operative Union's Central Education Committee and was a consistent champion of the Woodcraft Folk, as was Ted Hackett, who, in 1932, was appointed as the CEC's representative on Woodcraft Folk's National Council. Joseph Reeves saw the Folk as a great source of future strength for the co-operative movement, but he warned the current generation of youth not to be complacent about co-operation as it was practised in Britain and not accept the prevalent view that it was purely a business enterprise. In a withering attack on the political direction of the co-operative movement, he warned young people that

> they must not take co-operation for granted and must not accept the adults' view that it is wonderful achievement of working-class capacity for business building. [youth] will see that the Co-operative Movement falls short of Co-operative ideals in a lamentable manner, that there is less Co-operation among Consumers' Societies than there is among capitalist undertakings. They will ... wonder why societies are governed

by separately elected committees with no attempt being made to co-ordinate their work. They will see Education Committees doing work very similar to that undertaken by organisations receiving the patronage of the wealthy and they will be surprised at the way this great movement hastens to show its veneration for ancient institutions of privilege and exploitation.[3]

In his support for the Woodcraft Folk, Reeves had a more progressive future orientation of the co-operative movement in mind.

The co-operative movement did not see things in the same way. Although for most of the 1920s and 1930s relations were good, and the Folk was generally regarded as an auxiliary organisation of the Co-operative Union, it did not receive much in the way of what it needed most - money. As early as 1932, the Folk began to express its frustration at the lack of financial aid and was, in the end, reduced to sending a letter to the Educational Executive of the CEC (read out at the meeting) in which it recorded

> its deep regret at the failure of the Central Education Committee to grant it the financial assistance commonly accorded to auxiliary co-operative educational organisations.

The letter went on to remind the CEC of the 'important pioneer nature' of the Woodcraft Folk's work which provided the only alternative

> to the powerful non-co-operative and semi-militaristic organisations for children which count their membership in hundreds of thousands ... and ... that a pioneer movement, 75 per cent of whose members are under 16, should be deserving of their special charity.[4]

Financial Appeals

This and earlier appeals were supported by a number of local co-op societies and their education committees,[5] but appeared to fall on deaf ears. The Education Council refused even to pay the expenses of its own representative to the Woodcraft Folk Summer Camp of 1932.[6] Clearly it was the mighty Co-operative Union rather than its Education Committee which was calling the tune on this issue. In an unusual intervention the General Secretary of the Co-operative Union wrote to the Education Executive[7] stating that although the Executive Committee (of the Co-operative Union) gave £10,000 per annum to

43

fund the work of the Education Committee, this did not mean that the committee was free to use the money as it liked and that it must 'obtain the sanction of the Executive before making a grant to any outside organisation'. In regard to the grant to Woodcraft Folk 'after very full consideration of the whole circumstances, the Executive Committee could not agree to the proposed grant being made'. The Education Committee protested at this and asked for the decision to be reconsidered. It sent its representative (Mr Cox) to plead the case of Woodcraft Folk. He said the Folk grant was to be used for 'purely educational work which was considered to be of value as auxiliary to the work of the Education Department'. He pointed out that since 1929 Woodcraft Folk 'had been recognised as performing useful work in the way of attracting young people to the movement and he frankly admitted that it was doing work which the Education Department had failed to do.'[8]

The result of all this lobbying was the renewal of a £10 grant - hardly the generous response which one might have expected to be accorded to an 'auxiliary organisation'. Indeed, it was not only the Folk which perceived the sum as niggardly. The Education Executive regretted the Executive Committee decision and wrote at least twice during 1934 to protest. During the following year (1935) a series of rallies was organised in support of the Folk by individual co-operative societies, and in 1936 a number of conferences were held or planned jointly with sectional education committees and Woodcraft Folk. Basil Rawson was the main speaker at one such conference held in Sunderland in February 1936 which attracted about 100 people.[9] Perhaps it was this kind of support which induced the National Folk Council to assert that the Woodcraft Folk had gained 'enhanced prestige' in the co-operative movement.[10] This kind of local support induced the Folk to try again to break down the national barrier. Late in 1936 the Folk wrote to the Education Executive requesting a constitutional change to enable it to be entitled to representation on the National Education Council and that a grant of £100 per annum be approved for the purposes of contributing to the salary of a National Organiser. Whilst the first request was deferred for further consideration, the Education Executive could not 'hold out any hope'[11] that the latter would be granted.

By 1937 the Folk's frustration at its co-op parsimony induced it to resort to the expedient of distributing a leaflet to all the delegates at the Co-operative Union annual conference.[12] It rhetorically asked delegates whether they knew that 'co-operative woodcraft' organised children and young people, served world peace and supported co-operation and yet, (in capital letters and underlined), 'receives only £45 every year from the Co-operative Union and the CWS combined'. (The CWS being the Co-operative Wholesale Society.)

Thus far, it can be seen that relations between the two organisations, although supportive at a local level, were distant and unhelpful nationally, despite the efforts of Joseph Reeves and Ted Hackett, both of whom were members of the Central Education Committee and its executive for most of the period, and both of whom were staunch Folk supporters. Two reasons can be offered in explanation. One, as mentioned earlier, was the Co-operative Union's dislike of Woodcraft Folk's autonomy. This was clearly in evidence well before the big show down in 1946. In 1938 R A Palmer, General Secretary of the Co-operative Union, wrote to the Woodcraft Folk objecting to its members pledging themselves not to fight for 'King and Country' (see chapter 6) - a sentiment which is:

> entirely contrary to the accepted policy of the Co-operative movement .... The Executive Committee [of the Co-operative Union] repudiates entirely any association with this statement and protests against it being published by any body claiming association with the Co-operative Union.[13]

Political Friction

In another letter,[14] not recorded in the Co-op minutes, but preserved in the Woodcraft Folk files was an objection to the Folk describing itself as a socialist organisation 'especially in a paragraph in which the Folk is described as an educational auxiliary of the Co-operative Union.' Leslie Paul, although no longer Headman, replied to both these letters on behalf of the Folk. He played down the pacifist policy and pointed out that it had been adopted in 1934 and appeared only in the explanatory foreword to the Folk's constitution and does not comprise a membership pledge. He explained that the term 'socialist' is not used in any party political sense'[15] but only because of the Folk's affiliation to the Socialist Education International. The real issue for Paul was the question of autonomy. In a exasperated and rhetorical question he sought confirmation on whether 'auxiliaries shall not be permitted to express views at all at variance with the policy of the Co-operative Union.'[16]

Another indication of this political sub-plot behind the education executive's animosity to the Woodcraft Folk is to be found as early as 1938 in a memo[17] from the Co-operative Union's youth organiser discussing the future of the BFCY and Woodcraft Folk. He stated that he did not consider the latter to be necessary to the co-operative youth movement and having visited many Folk groups he found that there is nothing they did which could not be done by existing co-operative youth organisations - Junior Circles or Comrades Circles. However the memo reveals his suspicion that although there appeared to be little education activity on group nights, having been pre-warned of his visits, group leaders, contrary to their usual practice, refrained from giving talks. Judging by the 'very political' stance of *The Helper* and the publications of the Socialist Education International (to which the Folk was affiliated), he was sure that the normal practice at group nights (hidden only for his benefit) was to deliver a political message to the children. He went on to say that he thought that the '... attitude of the Woodcraft Folk to the Scout and Guide movement is a mistake ... and ... that there is not the evil in these organisations which is suggested by Woodcraft Folk'. It was his view that everyone must work together regardless of political or religious denomination. He noted portentously, but without comment, 'It is understood that the Roman Catholic Church has advised its members not to allow children to join the Woodcraft Folk'. Thus whilst not overtly casting the Folk in the role of a politically subversive organisation, there is enough in this memo and in the more open 'communist front' charges against the BFCY, to indicate that the education executive's desire to re-organise and control the left wing youth movement was politically motivated.

The other reason for the Co-operative Union's frostiness towards the Folk centred around its grand plan, announced in 1939, to unite all 'co-operative' youth and children's organisations into a new organisation which would include the British Federation of Co-operative Youth, the Children's Circles and the Woodcraft Folk. The policy adopted by the education committee was

> That there shall be a national Co-operative Youth Organisation with headquarters at Holyoake House, Manchester, the organisation being in two sections, Junior and Adolescent; the former being on the lines of the Woodcraft Folk activities, aiming at teaching co-operation through interest activities. The adolescents to be a contiguous organisation designed to be a training ground for eventual progress into existing adult organisations.[18]

The annual delegate meetings of both the Woodcraft Folk and BFCY rejected these proposals, although both organisations were asked to articulate their specific objections and consider how they could be overcome. The whole project came as a surprise to the Folk, since in 1936, the Education Executive of the Co-operative Union had been pursuing a different course. It had suggested that a National Youth Council, consisting of Woodcraft Folk and BFCY, be established. Both organisations responded favourably to this idea and were engaged in consultation about the details. It was entirely preferable to the National Youth Organisation proposal since this would destroy the Woodcraft Folk as an independent organisation. However, it also became clear that the 1939 proposal was also designed to destroy the BFCY. It would seem that this organisation had fallen out of favour with the parent body not only because it disagreed with their proposals for new co-op youth organisation, but because the BFCY's politics were not to the liking of the Education Executive. The BFCY was charged with 'the dissemination of Communist Party literature' and that its links with the British Peace Assembly were 'entirely at variance' with the policy of the Co-operative Union.

Later, after the war, the successor to the BFCY, confusingly named the British Federation of Young Co-operators (BFYC) founded in 1942, repeated the same charge. In a pamphlet outlining the history of the organisation it said that 'the BFCY during the middle 1930s, in common with most other youth organisations, had been infiltrated by members of the Young Communist League'.[19] By June 1940, largely due to its refusal to suspend its anti-war activities, the Education Executive recommended that 'The Co-operative Union should no longer recognise the BFCY and that its connection with the Co-operative Union should cease'.[20] In fact this was not carried out. Instead the BFCY was obliged to give an undertaking that there would be a total repudiation of all support of communist activities. It is surprising that the only study of the BFCY[21] does not mention the Co-op's anti-communism in its relations with the BFCY, neither does it mention the expulsion threat itself.

National Co-operative Youth Organisation

Nonetheless despite this unpromising situation, Woodcraft Folk did not turn away from the co-operative movement and was anxious to take advantage of any possible compromise solution. In particular it advocated an arrangement whereby the Folk would become part of the new National Co-operative Youth Organisation established in 1941. There seemed little chance of this at first since the NCYO was designed to take over the functions of the Folk. It established a three age group structure, the first two of which roughly coincided with the Folk's

47

already established Elfins and Pioneers. (The Co-op's grand plan consisted of: Playways for the 7-10 age group, Pathfinders 8-15, Youth Clubs 15-18 and BFCY for 18-25). There was considerable protest within the co-operative movement over this youth plan from local societies. Indeed the issue was the subject of debate at the 1941 Congress of the Co-operative Union, with the Folk's friend Ted Hackett leading the opposition. This centred on the issue of whether, in creating a new national youth organisation it was necessary to scrap the Folk and the BFCY: As Hackett said 'there ought to be room in a great movement for two young people's organisations of more than 10,000 members to be included.'[22]

In replying to the debate L A Hurt, Chairman of the Education Executive gave assurances that there was no intention of doing away with these two organisations. On this basis, 'a tedious and wearisome series of negotiations'[23] continued, for the next two years, at the Folk's suggestion, to explore the relationship between it and the NCYO. The Education Executive's unhelpful response was to suggest that the only way forward was to incorporate the Folk into the new organisation[24] - hardly consistent with the position advanced by its chairman, L A Hurt, at the Congress. Indeed the 'high handed' attitude of the Education Executive and especially its chairman, was regarded by the Folk as the chief source of the difficulty and was spelt out in pamphlet form in a 'White Paper'.[25] Nonetheless, the Folk proposed a compromise in which it rejected the NYCO but suggested that it become part of a National Co-operative Youth Council, that the co-operative representatives on Folk Council be increased and that decisions of the Folk's Annual Delegate Conference be submitted to the Congress of the Co-operative Union. Thus the Folk, whilst maintaining itself as a separate organisation would clearly have surrendered much of its autonomy. However, this did not prove acceptable to the then prevailing 'all or nothing' mentality of the Education Executive which regretted that the Woodcraft Folk 'desire to remain an independent organisation outside the Co-operative Union Youth organisation'.[26] Two months later the Education Executive recommended non renewal of the annual grant to the Woodcraft Folk.

This might have been the end of the matter were it not for the fact that the Woodcraft Folk had such strong local support within the co-operative movement. Individual co-operative societies continued to press the case for an amicable resolution of differences and this resulted in a resolution to that effect being carried at the 1942 Congress. The result of this was that in October the Folk was invited to meet the Education Executive 'for a full and frank discussion by both sides on the whole matter'.[27] At this meeting Basil Rawson stated that the Folk still worked closely with the co-operative movement at local level and 'would prefer to become part of the National Co-operative Youth Movement if a satisfactory basis could be found'.[28] Surprisingly, by 1943 a draft agreement was concluded. The fact that it was agreed by the Woodcraft Folk is even more amazing given that at the last minute the Education Executive threw in two caveats, one of which obliged the it to relinquish Folk House after a year of the operation of the agreement. Nonetheless the agreement was signed in 1944.

Given the Woodcraft Folk's historic determination to maintain its autonomy it is hard to understand how it could have accepted the 1944 agreement which effectively destroyed it. The Folk was allowed to retain its name and be represented as an organisation on local, district, sectional and national co-operative youth committees. It retained its own democracy, but its decisions could be over-ruled since in all other respects it lost its autonomy. On the plus side an Assistant Youth Organiser (Henry Fair) was to be appointed 'specially earmarked for work among Woodcraft groups' and *The Helper* became a printed monthly for circulation to all NCYO groups. Perhaps the most credible explanation for, what on the face of it, seems to be a liquidationist position is to be found in the difficult situation facing the Woodcraft Folk during the second world war when it suffered a severe depletion in its ranks and a great downturn in activity.

Whatever the reasons behind the decision of the Folk's leadership to become part of the NCYO, it is clear (in hindsight at least) that the arrangement was bound to fail, unless the Folk, like the BFCY, in submitting itself to the edict of Holyoake House, was to sink. When, in 1946, the folk took a decision with which the Co-operative Union disagreed, the relationship between the two organisations was put to the test in a David and Goliath contest in which, unlike the biblical version, Goliath, in the form of the Education Executive, was victorious (in the short term). The issue centred around the Folk's decision to organise an International Camp in Brighton in 1946. This remarkable camp was organised to include what remained of the European Red Falcons groups which like the Folk had been affiliated to the Socialist Education International - before its destruction by the Nazis. The Education Executive took exception to this on the grounds that '... certain organisations were included which could not be accepted by the movement as *bone fide* Co-operative organisations'[29] and that according to L A Hurt 'International contacts have been maintained and/or resumed, entirely independent of the Co-operative Youth Organisations and regardless of whether such contacts are acceptable to the Co-operative Youth Organisation as authorised by Congress'.[30]

Expulsion

The Folk was at pains to point out that most of the national Red Falcon groups were strongly supported by the co-operative movement in their own countries and that the British Co-operative Union had raised no objection to the Folk's affiliation to the International Falcon Movement's predecessor (the Socialist Education International) hitherto. Clearly the issue was one of central control: the Co-operative Union was not prepared to permit any initiative which it had not authorised and executed itself. The Folk was instructed to call off the camp and warned that unless it did so, notice would be given to terminate the 1944 agreement. For its part the Folk refused to cancel the camp and as a consequence the Education Executive ended the agreement and expelled the Woodcraft Folk from the NCYO. This provoked a storm of protest within the co-operative movement and wider. In June and July of 1946 a flurry of correspondence was despatched by the Folk to co-operative and labour movement organisations in the name of Reg Robson (the camp organiser) and Basil Rawson (Folk Headman) urging support for the camp and pointing out the injustice of the decision of the Education Executive. Rawson and Robson argued that they had gone through the proper channels and had approached the International Co-operative Alliance (ICA), but the latter had refused to put them in touch with any continental co-operative children's movement.[31] In a letter specifically addressed to the secretaries of local co-operative societies and education committees, the Folk complained of the 'high-handed' action taken and was sure that

> the rank-and-file co-operator will be disgusted at the method proposed to be used to enforce the children of the Woodcraft Folk to isolate themselves from their Continental comrades so soon after a war which we believed would mean the end of national barriers.[32]

Clearly this had some effect since the Board of Management and Education Committee of the Brighton Equitable Co-operative Society placed an advertisement in the *Co-operative News* opposing the disaffiliation of Woodcraft Folk without consultation with the movement and urging local societies to complain to the Education Executive of the Co-operative Union. Robson was quick to exploit this and circulated the text of the Brighton Society's advert with a request for similar action and a plea to notify him (by means of a tear-off slip at the bottom of his letter) should a protest be made.[33] However, despite the protests, the decision of the national Education Executive prevailed.

Undaunted the Folk went ahead with the International Camp of 1946. Inspired by its resounding success, the Folk looked forward with confidence and adopted a set of ambitious plans which in addition to seeking support from other labour movement organisations, also entailed employing two full-time officers. Henry Fair became National Organiser and Fred Kempton was appointed General Secretary. By 1949, however, the finances of the Folk were insufficient to maintain two members of staff and hence it was decided to dispense with the services of Kempton.

Apart from the publication of *Banned* in 1948, a pamphlet which aimed to tell the Folk's side of the story about its expulsion from the NCYO,[34] there was surprisingly little further debate in Woodcraft Folk circles over the expulsion issue. It seems that there was a determination to look to the future rather than pursue the sterile arguments of the past.

Reconciliation

In fact the termination of the national agreement made very little practical difference. The Folk had never been well supported financially at a national level despite its 'auxiliary' status. Its main benefit derived from its support by the local co-operative societies and education committees and this continued especially since, according to one historian of the RACS, the Co-operative Youth Movement (CYM) 'nationally went into decline after the mid-1950s' owing to 'its lack of purpose or identity, and its lack of a democratic structure'.[35] By 1969 it was officially wound up and its remaining members transferred to the Woodcraft Folk. This opened a period of harmonious relations between the two organisations which survives to this day, with the Woodcraft Folk recognised as the national co-operative children's organisation with a great improvement in the kind of practical and financial support for which Leslie Paul and Basil Rawson had campaigned.

Whilst they would undoubtedly have been pleased to see the cordial relations between the two organisations, it is doubtful whether, despite the increases, the financial support offered to the Folk ever matched its renewed status as a co-operative auxilliary. After 1969 the co-op could no longer use the excuse that it had its own youth organisation to support - Woodcraft Folk had the field to itself. However, by the 1970s both the CWS and the co-operative retail societies faced considerable financial difficulties and falling off of trading activities leading to the closure of many outlets and the amalgamation of local societies. Clearly in such straightened circumstances the cash grant to the Folk remained less than generous, although there were many other ways in which the co-op could and still does provide support.

Notes

1   Leslie Paul *Angry Young Man*, p143, Faber 1951
2   See Selina Todd's study of Comrades' Circles, 'Pleasure, Politics and Co-operative Youth: the interwar Co-operative Comrades' Circles' in *Journal of Co-operative Studies*, 32.2, September 1999: pp129-145
3   Alderman Joseph Reeves 'Woodcraft Folk and Co-operation', *The Pioneer* vol.3 no.9 April 1936
4   Minutes of Education Executive of the CEC, 20th August, 1932
5   Minutes of National Education Council, 18th March, 14th April 1932
6   This was the Mass Camp at Symonds Yat. A W Cox attended on behalf of the Co-op 'it being understood that no expenses will be incurred by this education executive' (minutes 18th July 1933)
7   Minutes of Education Executive, 18th November 1933
8   Minutes of National Executive of Co-operative Union, 20th January 1934
9   Minutes of Education Executive, 21st March 1936
10   Report of National Folk Council, 1936
11   Ibid 19th December 1936
12   The leaflet was inserted into June 1937 edition of the *New Pioneer*.
13   R A Palmer to Mr Mayston, 21st February 1938 (Folk House archive)
14   C E Wood, Co-operative Union Education Secretary to Mr Mayston (Woodcraft Folk), 22nd February 1938 (Folk House archive)
15   L A Paul to C E Wood, 5th March 1938 (Folk House archive)
16   L A Paul to R A Palmer, 5th March 1938 (Folk House archive)
17   Memo no.27, Youth Movement Archive/Woodcraft Folk/127
18   Minutes of Education Executive, 20th May 1939
19   E J Smythe *History of the BFYC* nd but probably 1948 (*BFCY at Your Fingertips* pamphlet no.4)
20   Education Executive, 15th June 1940
21   Selina Todd 'Pleasure, Politics and Co-operative Youth: the interwar Co-operative Comrades' Circles' in *Journal of Co-operative Studies*, 32.2, September 1999
22   Co-operative Union Congress Proceedings 1941 (second day)
23   *The Truth About Youth*, Woodcraft Folk, nd
24   Minutes of Education Executive, 20th September 1941
25   *White Paper on the negotiations between the CO-OPERATIVE UNION and the WOODCRAFT FOLK concerning the formation of a National Co-operative Youth Organisation 1939-1941*, Woodcraft Folk nd [1943?] YMA/WF/127
26   Minutes of Education Executive, 18th October 1941

27 Minutes of Education Executive, 16/17th October 1942
28 Minutes of Education Executive, 16/17th October 1942
29 Quoted in *Banned*, p4 - Woodcraft Folk pamphlet nd 1946
30 'Educational Executive Statement re Woodcraft Folk', Quoted in *Banned*, p13 - Woodcraft Folk pamphlet nd 1946
31 7th June 1946 YMA/WF/181
32 5th July 1946 YMA/WF/181
33 Undated circular YMA/WF/181
34 According to receipts filed in the Folk House archive, at least 57 co-operative societies and education committees requested bulk supplies of the pamphlet.
35 John Attfield *With Light of Knowledge - A Hundred Years of Education in the Royal Arsenal Co-operative Society, 1877-1977*, RACS/Journeyman Press, 1981

Chapter 5

THE LABOUR MOVEMENT, SOCIALISM AND THE FOLK

Throughout its history the Woodcraft Folk, with varying degrees of success, has sought to establish an organic link between itself and some or all of the main organisations of the labour movement. At the same time it has jealously guarded its own independence and autonomy and, as a children's and youth organisation, steadfastly refused to be party political although it never made a secret of its general socialist orientation.

Woodcraft Folk and Socialism

Until the second world war, the socialist politics of the Folk were, to say the least, overt. In the 1920s when the organisation was finding its ideological feet in an attempt to distinguish itself from its predecessors, its socialism was still overlaid with mystical romanticism. By the 1930s its socialist message was clearer. Paul described the Folk (in a somewhat exaggerated fashion) as in 'the van of leadership' for the creation of 'the new world order' in which the worker would be 'emancipated from his wage slavery and given economic power'.[1] For a supposedly non-political children's organisation the Folk was not only unafraid to nail its socialist colours to the mast, but to project an analysis based upon it.

In 1931 Leslie Paul offered his thoughts to the Folk on the national and international situation.[2] He noted the failings of the second (minority) Labour Government to tackle the pressing problem of high unemployment and wage cutting and offered a marxist explanation in which he noted that despite the tide of internationalism which had strengthened the working class movement in the immediate post-war years, capitalism, temporarily weakened, had renewed itself by 1926 so that it was able to re-assert its power and defeat the General Strike. The victory of capital had enabled the forces of the right in the labour movement to assert dominance once again. The defeat of the left and this drift to the right within workers' organisations was not confined to Britain, affecting, according to Paul, even communist countries like Russia and the revolutionary forces in China. The result of this world-wide trend was a renewal of nationalism and for him this meant the renewed threat of war. Having thus expounded his analysis, Paul felt obliged to explain what all this had to do with the Folk. He justified his polemic thus:

> When I was responsible for initiating the general policy of our movement, I proposed that there should be ... no trucking with imperialism or nationalism .... If we backslided on these questions then the justification for our existence would be gone .... Now we are one of the few movements which is sound on Imperialism.

He went on to say that because 90 per cent of the labour movement has no memory of 'the enthusiasm and idealism of the workers before their defeat in 1926', it was incumbent on the Folk to educate in order to build a better world - one that is based on a federation of nations co-operating together on a social basis. This vision was ardently supported by two Labour MPs who were Folk members: Reginald Sorenson and Fenner Brockway. A Labour Councillor in Birkenhead, B Birkett, wrote supporting Paul's vision of the Woodcraft Folk as 'a vital organisation in educating youth to become active in the labour movement in order to end capitalism and establish a new world order.'[3]

Woodcraft Folk and the Political Parties of the Left

Most political parties on the left (and on the right) in Britain have had youth sections, many of which have had a fractured history. At the time of the Woodcraft Folk's formation, the Labour Party had its League of Youth (1926), the Independent Labour Party[4] had the Guild of Youth (1924-32) and the Communist Party had the Young Communist League (YCL 1921). This is in addition to the various co-operative youth organisations (see chapter 4). Curiously though, much of the adult membership of the Folk came from these latter organisations. The question therefore is at once raised as to the nature of this paradox - namely that given the political orientation of the Folk's adult membership, the socialist orientation of the Folk and its link with the co-operative movement, why did the labour movement not give it more fulsome support? For Bernard Davies[5] the reason is to be found in the labour movement's pre-occupation with its own material interests which rendered 'leisure ... an arena of struggle of far less significance than the workplace, Parliament and the town hall'. It was predicated upon an assumption that the family wage (that of the adult male worker) was central to an improved standard of life and this, according

to Davies, resulted in the neglect of the needs of young people.
The Labour League of Youth

The Labour Party was, of course, the largest left of centre political party. Its League of Youth, catering for 16-25 year olds was explicitly non-autonomous. The Labour Party leadership's apparent reluctance to establish a youth organisation was overcome partly because of the fear of rival organisations like the Young Communist League.[6] Once the decision was made to have its own youth wing, it was clear that the Labour Party leadership intended to retain strict control. The formal position was stated clearly:

> The League of Youth is not an organisation separate from the Labour Party, but an integral section of its organisation. Its primary object is to draw young people into the ranks of the Labour Party ... As it is an integral section of the Labour Party, the League does not concern itself with questions of policy. These are discussed only at the Annual Conference of the Party.[7]

Furthermore the League was not permitted to affiliate or even co-operate with other organisations without first obtaining permission from officers of the Labour Party 'to ensure that the co-operation with such bodies will not be in conflict with the work of the Labour Party.'[8]

It would be tempting to suggest that the reason for the coolness between the Woodcraft Folk and other labour movement organisations, was political. At times this must certainly have been true as in the case of the break with the co-operative movement. However, in 1936 the Labour Party, in a rare show of support sent a circular to all branches urging them to support the Folk. This was the time when the Folk's left wing politics were more overt than at almost any other time in its history. The Folk actively co-operated with all 'popular front' type campaigns on the issue of Spain and anti-fascism in which the Communist Party often played a major, if not a leading, role. Labour Party policy, motivated as it was by profound anti-communism, refused to participate in any form of 'popular frontism' and instead urged reliance on the ballot box to solve all problems, albeit a general election was not held until 1945. Thus it is hard to explain why the Labour Party chose this moment to urge support for the Folk. It may be that it regarded the Folk as a safer bet than its own League of Youth which, between 1935-9 was undergoing very good relations with the Young Communist League (YCL) to the extent that in 1935 the YCL proposed that both organisations should merge to form a united socialist youth movement.[9] According to the Communist Party of Great Britain (CPGB), the National Committee of the League of Youth supported this proposal and as a result it was disbanded by the Labour Party in 1939.[10] Whatever the reason for the Labour Party overture to the Folk, there is no indication that it yielded it very much, and certainly did not produce what the Folk needed most - money.

During the war years, Woodcraft Folk, like most other organisations, gave serious thought as to how best to reconstruct itself after the severe dislocations brought about by wartime conditions. Henry Fair produced a radical memorandum[11] in which he proposed far reaching changes in the Folk. Amongst these changes was the suggestion that efforts should be renewed to interest trade unions and the Labour Party in the work of the Folk. Unlike some of the other proposals in the memorandum, this one was followed up after the war. Discussions were held at national level with the TUC, the Labour Party and the Fabian Society. In 1947 Folk members were urged to follow this up at a local level and at the same time were reminded that Folk Law decreed that all members should join their respective trade union.[12] Amazingly this initiative appeared to yield results. In 1948 *Labour Youth*, the journal of the Labour League of Youth carried an article entitled 'Meet the Woodcraft Folk'.[13] The article described the Folk's work and orientation as 'co-operative and socialist in character', but added that it 'does not indulge in **party** political activities as it believes that this is not the function of a children's organisation'. The conclusion was therefore, that having passed the test of political neutrality and having been sanctioned as a 'recognised auxiliary of the Co-operative Union ... its work is warmly commended both by the NEC of the Labour Party and the TUC General Council', the Woodcraft Folk was promoted (temporarily) as a suitable organisation for the children of Labour Party members.

No secret was made of the use to which the Folk could be put: its role was to act as a 'feeder' to the League of Youth and to the Labour Party. Apparently the irony of supporting a non party political children's organisation with the intention of using it for overtly party political purposes, was lost on the League of Youth. Clearly the League was expressing the views of the parent organisation. Two years later, in 1950 the Labour Party finally got round to publishing a pamphlet recommending support for Woodcraft Folk.[14] According to the author (s) the fact that one and a half million children are organised in 'imperialist and militaristic movements' has 'long caused grave concern to many thinking socialists'. It went on to say that the Labour Party

NEC has rejected the proposal to form 'junior sections' because this would 'overburden the party machinery at the present critical period'. Woodcraft Folk was suggested as a satisfactory alternative. The Labour Party 'now officially recognised [Woodcraft Folk] ... as the appropriate one for our purpose, and earnestly commends its work to the attention of local parties'.[15]

The TUC

The Woodcraft Folk was less successful in its dealings with the Trades Union Congress (TUC), despite the hopes raised by the fraternal greetings sent by the latter to the Folk on the occasion of its 21st birthday celebrations in 1946 and the fact that a meeting was held between representatives of the two organisations in January 1947. Following this the Folk invited the TUC to send a fraternal delegate to the 1947 Annual Delegate Conference (ADC) and enclosed a copy of its constitution and standing orders[16] with an invitation. A protracted and unproductive correspondence ensued in which the TUC agreed to send a message of support to ADC, but refused to send a delegate.[17] The Folk then suggested that the TUC appoint a representative to sit on National Folk Council. They were favoured ultimately with a reply from Victor Tewson, TUC General Secretary, who wrote that while the General Council sympathises with the objectives of Woodcraft Folk, they

> do not see that any useful purpose would be served by a TUC representative on your National Council and they regret that in the circumstances they are unable to appoint a representative.[18]

Clutching at straws, the Folk made a last plea. The Woodcraft Folk was pleased to note that the TUC sympathised with its aims and on this basis appealed for help in financial and other ways:

> By giving publicity to our work in publications going out to the movement and by giving official backing to any appeal which we might make in the individual unions for support.[19]

In time honoured procrastinatory fashion, Tewson in reply to this letter,[20] asked for more information on what kind of publicity the Folk had in mind. He flatly refused financial assistance. Although the Folk supplied the necessary information in February 1948, that was the last of the matter; the correspondence fizzled out along with the Folk's hopes for any real support in words or deeds from the TUC. It had taken over a year to establish that the TUC had given Woodcraft Folk the brush off. This is surprising only in the context of the more positive stand taken by the Labour Party during the same period.

In the 1970s the Folk repeated its attempt to gain trade union support. In 1975 it had a stall at the TUC Congress and renewed its appeal for funding. During the 1970s and 1980s there was a small ripple of response, by far the most significant of which was the decision of UNISON, the public services union to support the Folk financially.

The Communist Party and the Young Communist League

The archives of the YCL and of the Youth advisory committee of the CPGB[21] hardly mention the Woodcraft Folk: a surprising fact given that many communists were involved in the Folk and some of them were in leading positions. Apart from its sectarian phase during the 'class against class' period (1928-31), when it shunned relationships with any existing labour movement organisations, the CPGB's attitude to Woodcraft Folk can only be deduced. In general it was benign, but at the same time somewhat inconsistent given the nature of the changes in the party's political line. The reason for the CPGB's apparent indifference to the Folk cannot be easily explained. It may be that the Party regarded the Folk as a children's organisation and hence when the CP surveyed the youth scene as it did from time to time the Folk was automatically omitted. It is possible, as Prynn[22] suggests that the CPGB saw the Woodcraft Folk as a utopian 'back to nature' movement. This would have been a difficult charge to sustain during the 1930s when the Folk was involved in many popular front type anti-fascist activities in which it often shared a platform with Communist Party or YCL members (see chapter 6).

There have been many times throughout the Folk's history when it was labelled by its detractors as a communist front organisation and was, as a consequence, the victim of 'red scare' tactics. This was particularly the case in the 1930s when the Folk was very active politically. The Roman Catholic newspaper *The Universe* described Woodcraft Folk as 'an organisation of distinctly communist tendencies'.[23] It was not unusual for Woodcraft Folk members to be seen selling the *Daily Worker* at public meetings, giving rise to complaints from members of the Labour Party.[24] In 1936 the Folk sent a delegate to an open style YCL congress, the main business of which was to discuss a Charter for Youth Rights.[25] This event was 'exposed' in a pamphlet by the right wing Economic League.[26] This pamphlet purported to be 'an analysis of the plans of the Communist Party for the

59

penetration and capture of certain British youth organisations'.[27] The Economic League alleged that a plan had been hatched in Moscow by the Communist International for the unification of all socialist and communist youth organisations in Britain and that John Gollan (General Secretary of the YCL) had named the organisations he had in mind: his list included the Woodcraft Folk. The Folk was also named by the Economic League as being part of the audience of over 70 when the 'YCL club' was opened in Sheffield in February 1936. None of this appeared to deter Woodcraft Folk members from working closely with communists, although Leslie Paul was highly critical of the 'communist line' and suspicious of popular front activities and what he regarded as communist sectarianism of the type that, in his opinion, had led to the failure of communists and social democrats to work together in Germany and hence to block Hitler's rise to power. Despite its participation in 'united front' type youth activities, the Folk at the same time was concerned to build it own youth wing - the Hardihoods. Sidney Pool (Hawkmoth), the editor of *Herald of the Folk* thought that it was a mistake to suggest that the only way to fight fascism was by joining a left wing political organisation since such groups serve their own needs and hence do not have the breadth of appeal necessary to mobilise youth.[28]

The YCL had an ambivalent attitude to the boy scout movement. Until 1933 it was implacably hostile to what it regarded as a militaristic and imperialist organisation. At the 1928 YCL Congress a special section was devoted to 'The fight against the Scout Movement' urging that its 'disintegration' should be a 'permanent daily task of the League'.[29] The resolution also called for a systematic campaign against all bourgeois youth organisations. Two pamphlets had been published by the YCL in 1927 attacking the scouts. One of them, *Baden-Powell Exposed*[30] was a reprint of the correspondence between Bill Rust (then YCL secretary) and Baden-Powell following an interview with the latter in the *Daily Telegraph* in which he made an appeal for additional funds for the scout movement in London for the purpose of 'counteracting the insidious efforts of Communists to inveigle the youth of the world'. Baden-Powell alleged that the order from Moscow was to destroy the scouts because 'they have found that a great obstacle to the impregnation of the poison of Communism among the youth of the world has been the Boy Scout and the Girl Guide movement'.[31] Hence the scouts wanted to raise the extra money in order to establish scout and guide groups in working class areas where, according to them, there was greater risk of communist infiltration.

Bill Rust wrote an open letter to Baden-Powell in reply in which he asserted that B-P had at last let the 'non-political' mask of the scouts slip, and had exposed the movement as a means of conveying Tory propaganda to young people. Baden-Powell was rattled and offered to meet Bill Rust so that he could set the record straight and 'talk things over'. His language was that of Mondism (the 1920s equivalent of social partnership championed by the TUC and one of the employers' federations following the defeat of the 1926 General Strike). In fact he even quoted Ben Turner's (TUC) plea to do anything 'that will prevent the sore of poverty from overwhelming our land and destroying our nation ... let us co-operate ... with the idea of improving the lot of all.'[32] Although Bill Rust agreed to meet Baden-Powell, he was not convinced by the toned-down message of the former and insisted that the only way to fight poverty was by building the communist party and the YCL. The other YCL pamphlet attacking the scouts in 1927 entitled *Be Prepared for War*[33] was 'an exposure of the Scout Association and similar attempts to militarise young workers'. Its claim, that 'the YCL alone really fights the Boy Scouts', clearly ignored the role of other progressive youth and children's organisations, especially the Woodcraft Folk. This can only be explained by the sectarian blind spot engendered by the line of the Comintern ([Third] Communist International) which encouraged affiliated parties to break with their own reformist labour movements and to establish separate working class organisations under communist leadership.

By 1933, however, this line had changed and the YCL Congress of that year was critical of the 'sectarian mistakes'[34] of the past. The main resolution stressed the necessity of engaging in mass work in unity with others. Strangely, though, the congress also resolved to build a pioneer movement for children, apparently oblivious of the fact that such a movement already existed in the form of the Woodcraft Folk. This was to be a uniformed organisation (grey shirts and red neckerchiefs) and was to be modelled on the scouts on the grounds that because the latter was so successful it followed that the YCL should 'adapt the methods of the Boy Scouts to our movement.'[35] This was not acted upon.

Federation of Progressive Societies and Individuals

It is possible that the Folk failed to capitalise on the albeit limited Labour Party gesture of 1936 because it occurred at the same time that Leslie Paul was pre-occupied with another political organisation - namely the Federation of Progressive Societies and Individuals (FPSI). Paul was the joint editor of the FPSI journal, *Plan*, from 1934-8, but more significantly Woodcraft Folk was listed as one of the FPSI

61

affiliated societies and Paul was the Folk's official representative. Also, according to Paul the FPSI 'appeared to recognise the Woodcraft Folk as the appropriate juvenile organisation and youth movement for its younger members'.[36] The FPSI (later known as the Progressive Society) was founded by H G Wells and the philosopher C E M Joad 'to promote contact and co-operation between societies and individuals working towards social and economic reconstruction, with a view to increasing the effectiveness of their efforts'.[37]

Among its list of 22 Vice-Presidents were counted some of the leading intellectuals and literary figures of the day - Aldous and Julian Huxley, Leonard Woolf, Bertrand Russell, Rebecca West, Vera Brittain, Kingsley Martin, A S Neill and Barbara Wootton. For Paul the FPSI provided the possibility of creating an alternative non-marxist common front of left parties and intellectuals. He was critical of the popular front which, according to him, 'owed its existence to the sinister conspiratorial talent of the Communist Party'.[38] For Paul, H G Wells 'had become the spokesman and thinker of almost the entire non-marxist left'.[39] The FPSI devised a set of demands which Wells regarded as the 'common denominator'[40] of all left programmes throughout the world. This included demands for production for use rather than profit, the abrogation of national sovereignty and its replacement by a system of world government, sex equality (including reform of the divorce laws, legalisation of abortion), abolition of restrictions on freedom of expression (including the ending of the Blasphemy Laws). In practice the FPSI fell far short of Wells' grand world strategy and instead held a weekly 'informative lectures' or Forum meetings, which, by 1938, it regarded as 'one of the most valuable features of the year's work'.[41] Apart from the Woodcraft Folk only six other organisations were listed as affiliates of the FPSI. These, apart from the Artists' International Association, were esoteric to say the least. The National Sun and Air Association, the Federation of Sun Folk, the Hampstead Ethical Society, The Modern Culture Institute and the National Society for the Prevention of Venereal Disease were not the most obvious forces to carry forward Wells' 'fundamental revolutionary strategy' of 'world reconstruction'.[42] However, the FPSI, having set itself against 'the old fashioned class war western communist [and] the easy futilities of insurrectionism'[43] did not formulate any alternative revolutionary strategy, and thus one is forced to the conclusion that it was little more than a talking shop.

Why was the Woodcraft Folk affiliated to the FPSI? There appears to have been little discussion about the decision, given that the FPSI was a tiny and little known organisation. The only reference to be found of it in Folk literature is in *The Herald of the Folk* in 1933.[44] In this the FPSI was described as an organisation which 'attacks the problems of the world in our spirit' and that contacts have been made with it because it 'appears to recognise the Woodcraft Folk as the appropriate juvenile organisation and youth movement for its younger members'. One is forced to the conclusion that the Folk's association with the FPSI was very much a product of Leslie Paul's passing political idiosyncrasies. Paul considered himself to be a socialist and a militant. His militancy, especially during the General Strike, had led him to be sharply critical of the leadership of the labour movement, but at the same time he was critical of the marxist alternative in the form of the CPGB and the Soviet Union. Clearly he was looking for an appropriate political outlet and for him the FPSI seemed to fit the bill. In it he found 'a level of serious debate it was difficult to find elsewhere at that time'.[45] However, this capacity for argument and debate was also the unmaking of the FPSI according to Paul who observed that it 'proved capable of arguing everything exhaustively and doing nothing resolutely.'[46] Ultimately Paul judged the FPSI a failure. In his view it was interested only in sexual freedom and talking about world socialism.

The War and the Cold War

As we shall see, the Folk's pacifism did not endear it to the mainstream labour movement during the second world war (see chapter 6). However, this did not apply to the Communist Party since it too did not support the war for the first two years of its duration due to the Nazi-Soviet Non-Aggression Pact signed in 1939. As a result of this the CPGB's line was that the war was an imperialist one, and hence neither side should be supported.[47] However, when the Germans invaded the Soviet Union in 1941, the line changed and the Party advocated full support for the war against fascism. Conscientious objection was utterly condemned.

In 1949 Woodcraft Folk, concerned at its own stagnation, established an internal investigation to establish the causes of it and to chart a way forward.[48] Its terms of reference were wide ranging, covering all aspects of the Folk's policy, structure, activities and traditions. Groups and individual members were invited to submit evidence on any or all of these issues. One district (or 'Thing' in Folk parlance) used the opportunity to complain about what it regarded as the pro-communist bias of the Folk. It alleged that this was 'displayed by numerous individuals, leaders and consequently by some groups, thus endangering the non-party attitude of the Woodcraft Folk'.[49] As evidence for this the District (Thing of the Forest) pointed to the fact that the Woodcraft Folk songbook contained communist songs, that some members wore red neckerchiefs on their Folk costume and that the red flag was frequently displayed alongside the Folk flag. It is difficult to know how widespread this kind of sentiment was among Folk members. Certainly it is the only testimony presenting this view presented to the Enquiry Committee and could have been dismissed as a 'red scare' panic were it not for the testimony of Basil Rawson. Rawson was certainly not anti-communist, but his evidence to the committee indicated that he thought it was time for the Folk to move away from the overtly left wing political culture which permeated it. It is worth quoting Rawson's views in full since they obviously exercised some weight because of his position as Headman.

There is no chance of survival in this country for a children's organisation either teaching politics ... or with official links with political parties. The present position of the Folk is invidious because, despite declarations that 'preclude' us from any form of political organisation, our literature, charter etc ties the organisation to political theories upon which not even its own adult members are agreed.[50]

He went on to argue that the Woodcraft Folk Charter should be abolished since this 'would remove one of the remnants of political conditions of membership to which our friendliest critics point' and that the Folk should affiliate only to 'technically useful' rather that policy making bodies. It would seem that the timing of Rawson's observations on the political future of the Folk was borne of the greater political caution exercised by most progressive organisations in the anti-communist climate generated by the recently started cold war. Several other submissions criticised the Folk Charter as outdated and not easily understood by child or adult member alike and thus it was not surprising to find that one of the recommendations in the final Report of the Enquiry committee was to drop the Charter, Declaration and Creed, the acceptance of which, until now, was a condition of membership.

It would, however, be mistaken to assume that dropping the Charter signified a new rightward, anti-communist phase in the history of the Folk. Its international record showed the opposite. It was unafraid at the height of the cold war to make contact with children's and youth organisations from the socialist countries (see Chapter 7) despite criticisms it may have had of those countries' governments. Neither was it afraid to criticise the shortcomings of social democratic politics nationally and internationally. The fact that the Folk did not have the dependent relationship on the Labour Party (in terms of funding), as did its International Falcon Movement counterparts on their respective socialist parties, was seen as an advantage by Basil Rawson:

> It has not always been of advantage to us to be regarded as the 'junior section' of a political party .... In England our organisation is regarded as a children's organisation for socialist education of the left, and so receives the support of different parties of the left; but we have found often that our ideals, basic socialist ideas were in conflict ... with our party backing ....[51]

The Post-war 'Communist Bogey'

Despite its clearly non-aligned politics, there were frequent attacks on the Folk for its alleged communist sympathies. This prompted greater caution during the post war period. Thus in 1950, National Folk Council warned one of the South London groups to delete the words 'Woodcraft Folk' from any future advert in the *Daily Worker!*[52] It was undoubtedly the case that a number of Communist Party members were also members of the Folk, however, there is no evidence whatsoever to suggest that their work in the Folk was directed by the CPGB. Two surveys of the British Youth Movement approved by the YCL National Committee in 1946 and 1951 and one report presented by the Youth Advisory Committee to the Executive Committee of the CPGB,[53] contained no mention at all of the Woodcraft Folk, despite listing virtually all other youth organisations including that of the co-operative movement (the CYM). If anything the Communist Party appeared to be more interested in the Boy Scouts judging from the attention it paid to publicising the cases of two leading YCL members who were also scouts. In 1954 Paul Greenwood (a Queen Scout) and Dick Etheridge (later to become well-known as a communist militant in the car industry) were expelled from the Scouts purely on the grounds that they were both communists. The case went to appeal and was even the subject of a debate in the House of Lords on a motion proposed by Viscount Stansgate (Tony Benn's father). This was a clear case of political victimisation, but it indicated also that Woodcraft Folk was not necessarily the chosen, much less the targeted organisation for communists! The charge of communist infiltration arose publicly in 1963 in a scurrilous article in the *Sunday Telegraph*[54] which alleged that a campaign was being waged from King Street (CPGB headquarters) to infiltrate the Folk. Woodcraft Folk issued a press statement to counter this charge in which it wondered, somewhat ironically why it had not experienced a great rush of membership applications 'which would normally follow a directive from King Street - communists normally being well disciplined in this respect'.[55] The statement went on to say that the Woodcraft Folk, 'unlike other organisations of the labour movement, has never found it necessary to judge a person's fitness by their "party tag"'. Later 'communist bogey' attacks, the most serious of which was in 1976, followed from Woodcraft Folk's greater participation in the Youth Service and its consequent receipt of state and local government funding. This is examined more fully in Chapter 8.

Notes

1 1929-30 Yearbook, editorial by L Paul the 'March of Man', YMA/WF/1
2 *Where Britain is Going?* 1931-2 Yearbook, ibid
3 *Which Trail*, 1931-2 Yearbook pp6-7, ibid
4 The ILP was disbanded in 1932 when it took the decision to merge with the Labour Party.
5 B Davies *Threatening Youth*, Open University Press, 1986, p95
6 This is the view of a Trotskyite member of the LLY, Pat Sirockin in *The Story of Labour Youth*, Keep Left Pamphlets, Scarr [1960]
7 *The League of Youth*, Labour Party 1931, p1
8 Ibid p8
9 YCL archive (NMLH), CP/CENT/YOUTH/02/14
10 Ibid. After the NAC of the LLY was disbanded, Ted Willis, the LLY's National Organiser, and his supporters joined the YCL. The next Annual Conference of the LLY was not held until 1951.
11 Memorandum on the reconstruction of the Woodcraft Folk to meet post-war conditions, 1943, YMA/WF/13
12 Circular to all members on contacts with the labour movement, 6th January 1947, YMA/WF/138
13 December 1948, vol.1 no.38. This journal, previously named *Socialist Advance* from its post-war re-introduction in 1946, was to revert to its original pre-war name, *Advance* in January 1948.
14 *Labour Youngsters*, nd but probably 1950, YMA/WF/139
15 Ibid
16 Letter 20th February 1947, YMA/WF/137
17 Letter from George Woodcock (TUC Assistant General Secretary). 28th March 1947, ibid
18 Letter from Victor Tewson to WF, 27th October 1947, ibid
19 Letter to TUC, 5th December 1947, ibid
20 Letter from Tewson, 23rd December 1947, ibid
21 Both at the National Museum of Labour History, Manchester

22   David Prynn *The Socialist Sunday Schools, the Woodcraft Folk and Allied Movements: their Moral Influence on the British Labour Movement since the 1890s*, unpublished MA thesis, University of Sheffield, 1971

23   5th February 1937. Quoted in David Prynn op cit p332

24   D Prynn, ibid

25   CP/YCL/1/6 (YCL archive, National Museum of Labour History)

26   *Communism and British Youth*, June 1936, Economic League

27   Subtitle of the above

28   'Hanging the Hardihoods', *Herald of the Folk* July 1934

29   Report of the 5th National Congress of the YCL 1928, CP/YCL/1/2

30   CP/CENT/YOUTH/0410

31   *Baden-Powell Exposed* p3, op cit

32   Ibid pp6-7

33   *Be Prepared for War*, J L Douglas, CP/CENT/YOUTH

34   Report of the 7th National Congress of the YCL 1933, CP/YCL/1/4

35   Ibid

36   *The Herald of the Folk*, December 1933, YMA/WF/31

37   C E M Joad in *Manifesto: The Book of the Federation of Progressive Societies and Individuals* ed C E M Joad, p21, Allen & Unwin, 1934

38   L Paul *Angry Young Man* op cit p238

39   Ibid p239

40   H G Wells Introduction: There should be a common creed for left parties throughout the world in *Manifesto: The Book of the Federation of Progressive Societies and Individuals* op cit p14

41   *Plan*, no.10, vol.5, October 1938

42   H G Wells *Introduction* op cit p14

43   Ibid p15

44   *The Herald of the Folk*, December 1933, YMA/WF/31

45   L Paul *Angry Young Man* op cit p241

46   Ibid

47   Needless to say this 'volte face' in the CPGB's line, which seemingly sacrificed its anti-fascism on the altar of Soviet foreign policy, was not welcomed by all communists. It resulted in the resignation of Harry Pollitt from his post as General Secretary because he could not accept the new policy.

48   *Enquiry Committee into the Lack of Progress of Woodcraft Folk Since the War* YMA/WF/216

49   Ibid

50   Ibid

51   Discussion contribution from Basil Rawson, report on 'The Future Work of the IFM' Conference 1966, p7, YMA/WF/168

52   NFC 7/8th October 1950, YMA/WF/26

53   The 1946 survey was part of *YCL Club Leadership Course*, CP/YCL/11/1. The 1951 report titled *The British Youth Movement* was dated 21st July, CP/YCL/11/2. The 1952 survey presented to the EC of the CPGB was headed *Notes: For Discussion on the Youth Movement*, CP/CENT/YOUTH/02/13

54   7th July 1963

Chapter 6

PACIFISM, ANTI-FASCISM AND THE SECOND WORLD WAR

The left in Britain faced a dilemma in the inter-war period. On the one hand, the horrors of the first world war had, as we have seen, stimulated a strong inclination for peace, internationalism and above all disarmament. However, on the other hand, the fascist seizure of power in Italy (1922) and Germany (1933) brought the pacifist stance into question. The strength of the anti-war mood was clearly manifested in mass support for the League of Nations as the only organisation likely to prevent a recurrence of war. The League of Nations Union organised what came to be known as the 'peace ballot' which turned out to be the largest poll (apart from general elections) ever to be conducted in Britain. In all eleven and a half million people voted in response to five quite detailed questions relating to international arms reduction, the attitude to the League itself, the possibility of collective military security and/or economic sanctions and the banning of private arms sales. This was not simply a pacifist ballot but a clear statement of opinion on the way in which peace could be maintained. The overwhelming view was in favour of peace through collective security mediated by the League. By a strange quirk of fate the ballot results were announced in 1935, the year in which Mussolini invaded Abyssinia. Woodcraft Folk supported the peace ballot and published an article by its organisers in *The Pioneer*[1] and was represented on the deputation to the Prime Minister when the ballot results were submitted.

Despite the great hopes placed on it, fascist breaches of collective security had shown the League of Nations to be a blunt instrument. Clearly the League was only as strong as its member states permitted it to be, as the British example clearly showed. Baldwin's Conservative government signed the Anglo-German Naval Treaty in 1935 by which the Nazis were given the go-ahead to build 35 per cent of the naval tonnage of the British Empire. At this stage Western governments' pre-occupation with anti-Sovietism outweighed their concern with fascism.

The history of the Woodcraft Folk history mirrors the predicament of the British left and progressive movement - how to retain a pacifist perspective while at the same time being committed to the anti-fascist struggle. The Folk's pacifism was a central core of its being, reflecting the views of Leslie Paul who candidly admitted that he 'thrust the Woodcraft Folk into close contact with all the pacifist elements we could reach' and that he 'tried to turn the movement into a dedicated group of war-resisters'.[2] He went on to acknowledge that this position was not entirely consistent with his view that the Soviet Union had the right to defend itself against attack from the capitalist countries. Early on, in 1925 or 1926 the Folk had affiliated to the No More War Movement (NMWM). The contact with this organisation was through the Independent Labour Party, two of whose prominent members, Reginald Sorenson MP and Fenner Brockway, had children in the Folk. The No More War Movement was the successor to the No Conscription Fellowship. This latter was founded during the first world war, when in 1916 conscription was introduced for the first time in Britain. In the same year, however, parliament formally recognised the right to conscientious objection. In 1921 the No More War Movement took over from the No Conscription Fellowship and campaigned 'with all those who seek to remove the causes of war and to replace the war-breeding civilisation of the present time by a new Social Order based on co-operation'.[3] The NMWM was constituted as the British section of the War Resisters International, (a pacifist organisation with branches in most European countries and the USA), hence explaining 'the particular purpose of the Movement' which was 'to inculcate the principle of Resistance to War under all circumstances'.[4]

Woodcraft Folk's international contacts through the Red Falcon movement and its later affiliation to the Socialist Education International (see Chapter 7) brought it into contact with fascist reality early on. The fascist menace had a profound effect on the Folk politically and organisationally. The Austrian Red Falcons with whom Paul had especially close contact had sent a delegation to the 1933 mass camp at Symonds Yat, but by the following year, following the 'Anschluss', the Nazis had banned all progressive organisations, including the Falcons, and imprisoned their leaders. Thus the Folk's 1933 annual report noted the 'very serious situation' in Europe[5] and posed the question as to whether the emphasis of Woodcraft Folk should be on child training or youth activity of an overtly political nature, the aim of which should be to inculcate understanding of exploitation which would be the only sure basis for generating the beginnings of a socialist consciousness among youth. At this stage the Folk's pacifism was highly political: it regarded imperialism and capitalism as the cause of war. It would appear that the Folk had argued this point within the No More War Movement to which it had been affiliated for about five years. In 1933 the Woodcraft Folk annual report expressed its delight at the fact that 'the No More War Movement moves to the left'[6] and boasted that the No More War Movement had fully endorsed 'the direct pacifist education of youth through the Woodcraft Folk'.[7] Indeed in 1933 the NMWM published an article on the Folk in 1933 in their paper *The New World*. By 1934 the ascendancy of fascism in Germany and Austria, the threat of German Rearmament and the possibility of a civil war in Spain led Paul to suggest that the Folk now faced a stark choice: whether to carry on in 'our serene way as a small hopeful organisation' wishing that fascism would go away or to make anti-fascist work the main priority even though doing so would mean 'fighting the inertia of the co-operative movement and the labour party'. Unsurprisingly, Paul advocated the latter choice, but cautioned that taking it would mean a great change in the style of work of the Folk. He advocated that much of the mystical rituals inherited from Kibbo Kift should be dropped. This included jettisoning Indian names and the fringed jerkin style costume. Instead he advocated a more simplified green hiking suit for the pioneers and a blue shirt for the Hardihoods to be worn as a 'mark of respect for the smashed socialist youth movements of the continent'.[8] The Hardihoods were to be a new over 16 youth section (agreed at the 1933 Althing), the aim of which was to attract young people in working class areas who might otherwise be attracted to Mosley's blackshirts or other anti-socialist organisations. This initiative was influenced by the presumption that the Nazi coup in Germany had led to a belated recognition by the labour movement that children's and youth organisation was very important. In other words Paul, at this stage, was intent on creating a mass, politically conscious (albeit not party-political) children's and youth movement, which he suggested could build to 20,000 members in no time. This, of course, would have been a very different kind of youth movement, sharply breaking with the Seton tradition. For Paul this was a necessary step since the rise of fascism in Germany now led him to question the very essence of the Woodcraft Folk and scouting tradition. He had been told by Rolf Gardiner[9] that the pre 1933 mass German youth movement, the Wandervogel had readily embraced national socialism and had been transformed into the Hitlerjugend (the Hitler Youth). Was this merely a historical accident or was there something innate within such youth organisations which readily identified with the apparent iconoclasm of fascism and its appeal to physical perfection?

> I had to make another reading of my own past. The experiences of young men like me in Scouts, Kibbo Kift, Woodcraft Folk and other similar organisations were not so dissimilar from those of the Wandervogel. We shared with

them the rejection of European civilisation and the hope of a new, and in a sense more primitive one.[10]

Although some of these searching questions were raised much later in his life, an article Paul wrote at the time[11] expressed some of his misgivings about the German youth movement. In it he noted that even as early as the 1920s some of the German youth leaders were anti-semitic and reactionary. It is clear that Paul's detestation of fascism was the primary motive in his attempt to steer the Folk away from its cultish beginnings into becoming an organisation which firmly engaged with the current realities of life - especially the fight against fascism. In the days when the only consistent lead in the anti-fascist movement came from the Communist Party with its call for a united front, Paul was at pains to point out that the kind of anti-fascist work he advocated did not mean that he was pro-communist - indeed he was sharply critical of the failure of the German Communist Party (KPD) to make common cause, electorally and on the streets, with the Social Democrats in an effort to block the Nazi Party. However, at this stage Paul, although critical of communism, was by no means hostile to it. A far greater problem was the issue of pacifism which took on a more controversial character when, at the 1934 Althing a motion was passed in which the Folk pledged itself 'not to fight for king and country and to use every means in their power to ensure the future for freedom and peace.'[12] At this stage this policy was problematic only in the sense that it could be used by the Folk's detractors to imply that it was an unpatriotic, far left organisation. Indeed this was one of the complaints levelled against the Folk in 1938 by R A Palmer, General Secretary of the Co-operative Union (see Chapter 4). The fact that the *Daily Worker* backed the Woodcraft Folk position can only have served to confirm the fears of the Co-operative Union. The paper argued that

> It would ... be hard to find a worse example of misdirected and harmful interference. What is it that the greybeards of the Co-operative Union Executive object to? Is it the anti-war part? Or is it anti-fascism?[13]

However, the article went on to point out that it was the 'King and Country' resolution which had angered the Co-operative 'greybeards' and that although the Woodcraft Folk position was understandable in view of the excellent work they did in combating the imperialist tendencies of the scout movement it was nonetheless the case that the Folk 'should express things better' and that 'perhaps their policy needs clarifying and elaborating.'

As we shall see, the 'King and Country' resolution became a great bone of contention when Britain finally went to war with Germany in 1939. However, it was clear, as an interesting debate at the 1934 Althing showed, that Woodcraft Folk policy was contradictory. Paul proposed a motion which expressed admiration for the Austrian resistance to the Nazis and called on the British working class to mobilise 'in particular the Hardihoods, so that in itself it may offer a youth front against fascism'.[14] The pacifist and less political position was debated in an amendment to this motion which argued that it was against Woodcraft Folk principles to take up arms and that the Folk's main contribution lay within its educational remit. Interestingly some of those supporting the amendment said that the motion was too political and as such would incur the wrath of the co-operative movement. Basil Rawson, opposing the amendment stated that if fascism triumphed in Britain the co-operative movement (and the Folk) would be destroyed. Thus in a nutshell, this debate expressed the dilemma of the left and progressive movement.

Paul, however, did not oversee the organisational changes he advocated. He announced his intention to relinquish the position of headman in 1933 due to illness which he described variously as a breakdown, an enlarged heart and a disordered digestive system. Basil Rawson, the new Headman, although differing from Paul in style, character and class, continued the same political and organisational line as Paul had advocated. In any case Paul continued as President and was thus still involved although not in the day-to-day organisational work.

Anti-war, anti-fascist activity

It would be wrong to exaggerate the impact of the Folk's political work in the 1930s. It was a relatively small organisation[15] (although larger than the Young Communist League) and was not overtly political. Thus any assessment of its contribution has to take account of these limiting factors as well as the uniqueness of its position as a children's organisation. This said, it is clear that it played as big a role as it could. It sent nine delegates to the National Youth Conference Against War and Fascism held in 1934 in Sheffield. The conference was attended by over 600 representatives from British youth organisations, peace groups and trade unions and was addressed by the Bulgarian communist Georgi Dimitrov. (Dimitrov had been accused by the Nazis in Germany of starting the Reichstag fire in Berlin in 1933, but after skilfully conducting his own defence he was acquitted.) The Sheffield Youth

Anti-War Committee organised a mass demonstration the day after Mosley had staged a rally in that city. Basil Rawson was one of the speakers alongside the veteran socialist leader Tom Mann, John Gollan (general secretary of the YCL, but speaking in his capacity as leader of the Youth Anti-war Movement), Sam McAskie (chair of the ILP Guild of Youth) and John Greenwood (Labour League of Youth). In 1937 Rawson was invited to become vice-president of the Sheffield Basque Children's Council. These two examples of Woodcraft Folk's inclusion in the peace and anti-fascist movements are testimony to Rawson's standing in his native town, but also imply a recognition of the work of the Folk.

The Woodcraft Folk and the Public Order Act 1936

In what was presumed to be an effort to curtail the activity of the British Union of Fascists who aggressively marched in areas with a high Jewish population, clad in their Nazi-style black uniforms and jack boots, the government introduced legislation (the Public Order Bill) which sought to ban the wearing of uniforms by political organisations. The Bill was drafted after the battle of Cable Street, where in 1936 the BUF, despite police protection, had been stopped from marching through the East End of London by a massive mobilisation of the Jewish community and the Communist Party. However, it became clear that the Act in practice was directed against political demonstrations of all kinds. The government appeared to be more concerned with banning anti fascist counter demonstrations than curbing fascist activity: no attempt was made to stop Mosley's BUF marching through Bermondsey in 1937.

One of the organisations immediately affected by the ban on uniforms was Hargraves' Green Shirts, but the act also had implications for the Woodcraft Folk. Stafford Cripps, a barrister and a Labour MP advised the Folk that they were likely to come under the ban because 'their aims ... are stated to be co-operative and socialist, and anti-war and anti-fascist.'[16] The Folk was therefore presented with a clear choice - it either had to modify its constitution and thus enable its members to continue to wear folk costume, or stick with the original wording and jettison the costume until the act was repealed. This apparently straightforward choice led to a complex debate in which an attempt was made to reconcile political expediency with political principle. Somewhat strangely, given the socialist orientation of the Folk, it was decided that it was more important to retain Folk costume than the constitution. The argument was that if the costume was dropped it would be hard to re-introduce it whereas altering the aims of the Folk was a temporary measure. Undoubtedly this position pleased those members of the Folk who believed that it was becoming too immersed in left wing politics. An article in *The New Pioneer*[17] expressed this view:

> There appears to be an increasing drift to communism in some sections of the Folk, which for a children's educational organisation is ... regrettable. Party politics of any kind should be kept out of our work ... I am not decrying communism, but ... it is most certainly not anti-war, it is without question an aggressive doctrine.

An article in *The Helper*[18] offered another explanation for retaining the costume and modifying the constitution. It suggested that the Public Order Act revealed the contradictions in Woodcraft Folk activity. The Folk, so the author argued, had been moving away from its original function as a children's organisation and had instead been concerned with attracting youth (the Hardihoods). If the Folk continued in this way it would be competing against such organisations as the Labour League of Youth and the British Federation of Co-operative Youth, and the result would be failure in the same way that previous woodcraft movements which moved away from children failed.

Although Leslie Paul would have not shared these sentiments at this time, he was concerned to ensure that Folk retained its political neutrality. This is what lay behind his advice to the Folk on how it should respond to the Public Order Bill. National Folk Council[19] resolved that 'no resolutions of a political nature' shall be accepted for the agenda of any Woodcraft Folk body and that members should not be permitted to engage in any political activity whilst wearing Folk costume. The aims of the Folk were to be re-drafted with a greater stress on its educational function. Furthermore, to meet the requirement of the Bill, Paul proposed an 'immediate inquiry into (the Folk's) national and international affiliations ... with a view to ascertaining to what extent these commit us politically'. These measures were made somewhat more palatable by the assurance that they were to last for one year only and also by a statement adopted at the Annual Delegate Conference of 1938 which, while acknowledging that circumstances precluded it from direct political activity, went on to say:

> Woodcraft Folk affirms its view that political action is necessary to further working class interests and urges its youth

and adult members to undertake political activity in the appropriate working class political organisations and to become members of their appropriate trade unions and co-operative societies.[20]

Woodcraft Folk's anti-fascist and international work (in particular its organisation of and participation in international camps - see Chapter 7) excited the curiosity of Special Branch. Given the terms of the Public Order Act, Special Branch was particularly concerned about the 1937 international camp to be held in Brighton. Clearly Special Branch was in no doubt about Woodcraft Folk's politics which, in a secret memorandum, was described as 'in essence a socialist counterpart of the scouts' movement, but its avowed objects include active opposition to war and fascism.'[21] The same document recorded the fact that Leslie Paul had visited Russia in August-September 1931 and had been a delegate to a congress held by the British anti-war movement.[22] The Home Office wrote to A Maxwell, the Chief Constable of Brighton[23] advising him that uniforms may be worn 'on condition that no person wearing the uniform shall attend any meeting of a political nature or take part in a procession in the nature of a political demonstration.' However, the fact that foreign delegations to the camp were permitted to wear their uniforms (blue shirts and red scarves), aroused the ire of the fascists who raided the camp, stealing flags and banners. Henry Fair recounts that questions were raised in Parliament:

> Why were foreign Jews allowed to parade through the streets of Brighton with their red flags while patriotic British people were not allowed to wear their black shirts? So I had quite a lot of Home Office officials come down and I had to convince them it was not a political camp.[24]

Solidarity and refugee work

Given that most adult members of Woodcraft Folk came from political backgrounds: (the co-operative movement, the Labour Party, the Independent Labour party, the Communist Party and their respective youth wings), it was not difficult to mobilise them for anti-fascist solidarity work. The Folk was to be seen on most of the anti-fascist demonstrations, was active in raising money for Basque children during the Spanish civil war. Basil Rawson's invitation to become vice-president of the Sheffield Basque Children's Council was a clear acknowledgement of the solidarity work of Woodcraft Folk.

In October 1938 the leader of the Czech delegation (a friend of Willi Hocke, the IFM leader), at the International Camp (Brighton, 1937) visited Henry Fair to appeal for help to assist the emigration of Czech Falcon children, many of whose parents were in peril of their life. This appeal was precipitated by the infamous Munich agreement of 1938 when the British prime minister, Neville Chamberlain, pursuing his policy of appeasing fascism, colluded with Hitler's annexation of parts of Czechoslovakia (the Sudetenland). All progressive organisations were banned, including the Czech Falcon organisation. The Folk responded swiftly to the request for assistance. Henry Fair sent a circular[25] to Folk members asking them to take a Czech child into their homes. Prior to outbreak of the war, the British (appeasement) government was obstructive, insisting, according to Henry Fair, on a payment of a £200 bond for each child, a fee that was waived once the war began and the first 20 refugees 'children of socialists and trade unionists'[26] finally arrived at Victoria station as part of the remarkable Kindertransport from Czechoslovakia which saved the lives of 664 mostly Jewish children. The story is best told by Zuzana Medasova one of the 20 children of this first group to arrive in Britain. She recounts in *Rosh Chodesh* (1998), a magazine of the Jewish community in Prague[27] that monthly trains left Czechoslovakia in 1939 organised by a 28 year old English man then resident in Prague, Nicholas Winton:[28]

The children aged from a few months old up to their 16th year left this country in 1939 ... travelling the width of Germany in sealed carriages: I was one of the oldest girls and well remember the angry faces and clenched fists of the Germans standing on the railway platforms at Nurenberg and many other German towns ... my father was already in hiding from the Gestapo ... (he was) an Austrian socialist, political editor of *Vorwarts*, the daily paper of the Social Democratic Party of Germany during the Weimar period. Of course he had to flee at once - the paper was forbidden and its editors were enemies of the new state! So, together with many other anti-nazi refugees, both Jewish and non-Jewish, Czechoslovakia was their first place of exile ... Very soon the children of these refugees were formed into a youth group called DIE ROTE FALKEN ... and there were many red Falken Groups throughout Czechoslovakia, mainly in the German speaking parts ... Some of us Rote Falken had attended an International Youth Camp in the summer of 1937: it was held in England, near Brighton, I think the Czechoslovak group consisted of over 300 members ... none of us could guess that two years later Britain would become our new homeland.

The organisor (sic) of this large camp - the head of the WOODCRAFT FOLK - was a young married man, an idealist, keen trade unionist, humanitarian ... we all love this man. He was eager to know from our youth leaders what was then the situation in Czechoslovakia and he kept in touch with them after our return from this wonderful holiday. When it became obvious that the Germans had their eye on their Czech neighbours Henry Fair wrote a pleading letter to all members of the Woodcraft Folk, asking them to volunteer to take some of the children whose parents were once again threatened by the Nazis: it must be said that these were working-class families and that, by taking a refugee child, they would certainly have to make financial sacrifices ... none of us could imagine that we would never see our parents again ... in my case, out of 52 members of my mother's extended family only 8 survived - 2 returned from the horrors of Auschwitz and Belsen.

Clearly Woodcraft Folk, and in particular Henry Fair, quietly and persistently played a very important role in saving these Czech children from what would otherwise have been certain death at the hands of the Nazis. This explains why so many of the survivors hold the Woodcraft Folk in such high regard. For example Henry Bunzl, now living in a kibbutz in Israel, was one of the many who wrote movingly to Henry Fair over 40 years later to express his gratitude and recount the memory of his traumatic childhood 'metamorphosis' in 1939 from a Jewish middle-class Czech family (all murdered) into

> an English, Christian, poverty stricken family; dedicated to socialism, fighting the Blackshirts in the East End of London, and caring enough to undertake the raising of a refugee .... The memory of this has never (ever) left me. Though I have never found a way to express the tremendous gratitude I feel towards all of you in the Woodcraft Folk, who in fact gave me the possibility to live my life, and today to reflect on that period, not in sorrow, not in grief, but with pride that I too was part of the Woodcraft Folk.[29]

The importance of the Folk's work in saving Czech children is also verified in a negative way: Henry Fair was accorded the dubious honour of a place on the list of prominent anti-fascists wanted by the Gestapo.[30]

The Second World War and Conscientious Objection

Woodcraft Folk papers, publications and committee and other minutes say very little about the war itself, other than advising and reporting on structural re-adjustment to take account of difficult wartime conditions. At first this lacuna seems very surprising given that the Folk had policy and encouraged debate on all issues. Besides, what could be dearer to the heart of the Folk than the issues of peace and anti-fascism? The absence of policy and debate on the war can only be explained by the deep divisions that existed within the Folk on the issue - divisions which, had they been permitted to surface, would have rent the organisation asunder and may well have destroyed it. The only policy on the war was a decision not to have a policy. This was expressed in a motion proposed by Leslie Paul at National Folk Council in 1939 (September) and adopted by Annual Delegate Conference the following year. Paul said that the war placed the Folk in a difficult position: it could not declare for or against the war instead it must 're-affirm its faith in co-operation and socialism' and that it should 'stand by and assist all those adult members who reject military service.'[31] Thus the policy of refusing to fight for King and Country policy had not been rescinded, but once the war started in 1939 and men were required under the terms of the National Service (Armed Forces) Act of 1940 to register for military service, it was quite clear that many Folk members of the appropriate age group who responded willingly to call-up did not feel bound to carry out the Folk's pacifist policy. The war against Hitler created a distinction between pacifists as a matter of principle and those who were opposed to war. Such a distinction was not so keenly felt during the second world war - the war was opposed by all on the left as an imperialist war fought to re-divide the world among the great powers. The war of 1939-45 was viewed differently. This was seen as a 'peoples' war against the menace of fascism - a war that had to be fought and one in which the left had played a major part in initiating.

However, it was clear that a vocal group intended to carry out the Folk's pacifist policy to its ultimate limit and thus attempted to register themselves as Conscientious Objectors (COs). In one of the very few circulars issued on the war,[32] the national leadership of the Folk indicated the way in which it was to deal with this divisive issue:

> The committee felt that owing to the widely varying attitude of members within the Folk, it is nor possible or advisable to lay down a definite lead on this question [ie national service] but

there are no doubt many Folk members who through the peace teaching of the Folk, wish to object against service. For such persons it should be noted that **they should register their objection** when called up for registration at their local employment exchange ... our notice has also been drawn to a few groups who have passed resolutions expelling members because of their service in the Territorial Army. It is pointed out that no section of the movement have the right to expell (sic) members under Folk Law.

Despite the attempt at impartiality, it would, nonetheless, appear that on balance the main effort of the Folk during the war (apart from maintaining some level of activity as a children's/youth organisation), lay in supporting those of its members who became COs. Some prominent members of Woodcraft Folk were COs: perhaps the most influential of these was the National Organiser, Henry Fair (Koodoo). Fair cited his Folk work and the principles underlying it in his application for CO status. He stated:

> I have strong objection to taking part in any form of work or organisation that tends to promote or help in carrying out warfare and the taking of human life ... I know that all war is wrong and is a crime against humanity [He then recounts his disaffection with the youth section of the Labour Party which he joined after leaving school because of its non pacifist stance and thus he left it and joined the Woodcraft Folk.] since this organisation has its objects the training of children to work for world peace and world co-operation and a belief in International Brotherhood ...[I] worked ceaselessly for these objectives ... which entailed giving up all my spare time including holidays.[33]

In 1937 he gave up his paid work as a colour matcher since he 'refused to make paint for guns and bombs'.[34] Fair was unusual among Woodcraft Folk COs in that his application for CO status was agreed by the tribunal.

Other Woodcraft Folk pacifists were not so fortunate. Donald Rawson (Basil Rawson's son) and Reg Robson (Little Owl), had their applications rejected and as a result, following their refusal to attend an army medical, they were imprisoned. Much effort was made by individual Folk members to support the applications and appeals against sentencing of would-be COs. It was clear that the national organiser,

Henry Fair, spent much of his time in attending tribunals in support of Folk pacifists as did Margaret White (later to become National Secretary of Woodcraft Folk). The latter estimates that 25 per cent of eligible Folk members were Conscientious Objectors.[35] There was clearly a fine line to be drawn between committing the organisation as such to CO activities, as opposed to members acting in a personal capacity. This was expressed in a letter sent by Fair in 1943 in which he appealed for financial support for the work of the Central Board for Conscientious Objection.[36] He was careful to point out that this was a personal letter and not a Folk circular and that any cash received would be forwarded in the name of Woodcraft Folk COs and not on behalf of the Folk itself.

Despite such caution, it was clear that the Woodcraft Folk as an organisation was officially aligned with the CO movement - it was affiliated to the Central Board for Conscientious Objection. Other affiliates of the CBCO included the Society of Friends (Quakers), the Peace Pledge Union, the Independent Labour Party, the Women's Co-operative Guild and various church organisations. The CBCO was formed in 1939 as a product of the amalgamation of 17 national pacifist organisations. The Central Board saw its role as being the dissemination of advice, information and financial assistance - it did not 'undertake propaganda, recognising that each constituent body can best express its own particular faith'.[37]

It was also clear that many members of the Folk were unhappy with its pacifist stance. There is much oral testimony that those who accepted their call-up presented white feathers to those Folk members who did not. At least one member, W Quarterman, resigned from the Folk because he did not agree with its policy 'as regards objection to national service'.[38] The only occasion in which there was an attempt to democratically debate the war time policy of the Folk was at the Annual Delegate Conference of 1944 when Badger proposed the following resolution:

> That this ADC places on record its pride and appreciation of those Kinsfolk, men and women, who as members of the armed forces are engaged in the fight against Fascism and declares their actions to be fully in accord with the Folk's great anti-fascist traditions. It further declares that the survival of the Woodcraft Folk depends on a victory for the allies.[39]

However, despite strong objections from the floor, the motion was ruled out of order on the somewhat specious grounds that the Woodcraft Folk was affiliated to the CBCO.

Leslie Paul was opposed to the pacifist line of the Folk and joined up early on. For him the war against fascism changed everything: 'One could not be a pacifist if one longed with all the ardour of one's soul for the defeat of National Socialist Germany'.[40] Paul acknowledged the breach between his position and that of the Folk leadership. He felt that their rejection of military service was self righteous and incomprehensible given that 'they had seen their comrades in Germany, Austria, Czechoslovakia and Poland go down under the Nazi terror'.[41] In a letter to Henry Fair[42] written after his discharge from the army, Paul explained his reason for ceasing active involvement in the Folk. Paul was angry that the Folk had removed him 'with indecent haste'[43] from the presidency when he joined up. Furthermore the Folk had:

> Made haste to abolish the office I held and so cut me off from any official correspondence connected with the movement. As this was an act of the ADC [Annual Delegate Conference] I could not take it as other than the wish of the movement.

He went on to say that although he bore no ill-will to the organisation he founded and was happy to remain an individual member, he wanted Fair to read his letter to National Folk Council 'so that there can be no ambiguity about my position.'

Despite such divisions, the Folk nonetheless remained intact as an organisation during the war, although its activities were greatly reduced as a result of call-up, evacuation from the big cities (where the Folk was strongest) and war-time emergencies. Membership, unsurprisingly, fell.

Notes

1   May 1935
2   L Paul *Angry Young Man*, p124
3   NMWM leaflet, nd, International Institute of Social History (IISH)
4   Ibid. In 1937 The No More War Movement merged with the Peace Pledge Union, a peace organisation which had been formed in 1934 by the Reverend Dick Shepherd and included Aldous Huxley, Siegfried Sassoon, George Lansbury and Bertrand Russell among its sponsors.
5   Woodcraft Folk Yearbook 1933, YMA/WF 1
6   Article by Leslie Paul, Woodcraft Folk Yearbook 1933, YMA/WF 1
7   Ibid
8   L Paul *The Last Ten Years and the Next*, Woodcraft Folk Yearbook 1934, YMA/WF 1
9   Gardiner had been a member of Kibbo Kift and had subsequently spent

much time in Germany where he was involved in one of the largest youth organisations (Freischar). Initially he supported Hitler arguing that the new regime represented a triumph for German youth.

10   L Paul *Angry Young Man* p206
11   In the *Adelphi* magazine, March 1934, referred to in L Paul *The Early Days of the Woodcraft Folk*, Woodcraft Folk 1980
12   10th Althing: WF archive, Folk House
13   *Daily Worker* 2/3/38
14   Ibid
15   Although membership was growing slowly, according to WF Annual Report, by 1937 the total adult and child membership stood at 3,518
16   Letter from Stafford Cripps to Leslie Paul, YMA/WF/203
17   Vol. IV no.4, November 1936. The author's Folk name was Redwood YMA/WF/332
18   March 1937. The article is unsigned.
19   NFC January 30/31 1937, YMA/WF/26
20   ADC 8/9 January 1938, YMA/WF/26
21   The Woodcraft Folk: Wearing of Uniforms by Children 1937, PRO/MEPO 2/3103
22   Held at Bermondsey Town Hall 4/5 March 1932?
23   March 16 1937, PRO op cit
24   *We are of One Blood*, Woodcraft Folk 60th anniversary pamphlet, 1985, p20
25   1st November 1938
26   *We Are of One Blood* op cit p21
27   I am indebted to Paul Bemrose for providing me with this invaluable article and other information on WF and the Czech children which he obtained from the late Henry Fair.
28   According to Zuzana Medasova such was Nicholas Winton's modesty that his role in organising the Kindertransport from Czechoslovakia was unknown to a wider public until 1989 when he appeared on Esther Rantzen's *That's Life*. He has now been honoured as a 'righteous citizen' in Yad Vashem, the holocaust memorial in Israel.
29   Letter from Henry Bunzl to Henry Fair October 4th 1995. The family he refers to are the Bryants then living in Hoxton Square, east London.
30   This information, passed to me by Paul Bemrose, was discovered by Hsi-Huey Liang, Professor of History at Vassar College, USA. The latter discovered this in the course of his research at the Federal Archive in Potsdam on the kindertransport (ref: file R58/2335, RSHA, Amt IV, Geheime Staatspolizei, 'Emigranten der CSR'). Liang wrote to Henry Fair in 1995 informing him of the discovery!
31   NFC minutes YMA/WF/26
32   *New Conscription Act 1939*, YMA/WF/213
33   Correspondence concerning the registration of H A Fair as a CO YMA/WF/211
34   Ibid
35   Interview with Margaret White, August 2000

36 7th September 1943 'CO Week 19-26 September' YMA/WF/213
37 Central Board for Conscientious Objection pamphlet, (*The CBCO: Its Work and Needs*) October 1941, YMA/WF/213
38 W Quarterman to J Mayston, 12th August 1940, YMA/WF/199
39 1944 ADC minutes, WF archive
40 L Paul *Angry Young Man* op cit p284
41 Ibid p285
42 L Paul to H Fair 31st May 1946, YMA/WF/199
43 Ibid p274

Chapter 7

INTERNATIONALISM AND THE COLD WAR

Soon after its formation Woodcraft Folk made links with similar youth and children's organisations in continental Europe. However, it was not until 1935 that the Folk joined the international body to which many of its European counterparts were affiliated - the Socialist Education International (SEI), founded in 1924. Most of the national affiliates of the SEI, many of which were named 'Red Falcon' or 'Falcon' groups, were destroyed by the fascists between 1933 and 1945 and hence had to be rebuilt after the second world war along with the International itself, which, after 1946 was known as the International Falcon Secretariat, and from 1954, the International Falcon Movement (IFM). The Folk played a major role in reconstructing the IFM, although its later relationship with it was often stormy. All the pre-war archives of the SEI were destroyed by the Nazis. Nonetheless given the importance of the SEI and the IFM it is surprising that there has been no authoritative study of either or both.[1] This book will not attempt to remedy the deficit, although it is to be hoped that somebody will!

Why was it that the Folk took until 1935 to decide on affiliation to the SEI, and why anyway did it choose the SEI given that there were other international children's organisations in existence? These questions are hard to answer since no record exists relating to the internal discussions on these matters. Leslie Paul had, since the early days of the Folk, established contacts with the Kinderfreunde organisations (the origins of the Red Falcons) of Austria and Germany - both of which were very impressive mass youth movements. These two together with the Czech Kinderfreunde were the founder members of the SEI. It may be that the Folk was unwilling to involve itself in the political division of the left in Europe following the Russian Revolution. The SEI was closely associated with the Socialist Youth International (SYI), established in 1923 to counter the influence of the Communist Youth International (CYI) founded four years earlier. An example of the close links between the SEI and the SYI organisations may be found in the fact that the SEI journal appeared as a supplement of the SYI magazine *Youth Correspondent*. The SYI frequently accused its rival, the CYI, as being 'an agent of Moscow' and an 'annex of the Comintern'.[2] However, for its part the SYI was closely associated with the Socialist International (of Social Democratic and Labour parties).

This was a revival of the Second International (1889-1914) and functioned until the fascist conquest of Europe. It was reconstituted in 1951 as a reformist opposition to communism (the Comintern having been dissolved by Stalin in 1943). Thus the split in the socialist movement between communists and social democrats, the first sign of which had begun during the first world war, was complete by 1920 and continues.

The communist/social democrat split posed problems for many socialist organisations which did not want to be forced to take sides in their international work and which, like the Folk, prized their political autonomy. However, it is no accident that the Folk decided on affiliation to the SEI in 1935. In that year the Labour Party officially recognised the Folk, and hence the Folk was tempted to regard itself, albeit temporarily, as occupying a similar position to some of the continental youth organisations which were so closely linked to social democratic parties.

Whatever the reasons for joining it, the SEI was attractive only to the extent that it practised a form of internationalism which had some meaning to a children's movement. This was the case from 1933 until 1939 when the SEI embarked on the ambitious project of establishing, every two years, 'children's republics'. These were the means by which the SEI facilitated direct international contact between children and young people of different countries through the organisation of international tent camps. This fitted well with the determination to rid the world of war through the development of international understanding, to which the Woodcraft Folk was committed. The Folk sent a delegation to the first two SEI international camps (1933 Belgium, 1935 France). In addition it sent and received bilateral delegations at national camps. The Folk hosted the largest of the pre-war international camps in Brighton in 1937 (see Chapter 6). In 1939, on the eve of the war, an SEI international camp was held in Belgium (on the border with Germany) at Wandre-Liege. The Folk took a 900 strong delegation. This camp was, according to Leslie Paul 'a demonstration of European youth for peace and against fascism',[3] but at the same time it was, to use Paul's words again, 'a farewell to all those idealistic dreams of the twenties and thirties of the brotherhood of man and a better world. The international friendships we had formed were broken, some forever.'[4]

After the war the Folk's initiative in organising the international camp in Brighton in 1946 was not only a remarkable feat in itself, but was also significant in that it laid the basis for the re-foundation of the international movement. However, this was, as it turned out, a mixed

85

blessing.
Woodcraft Folk and the International Falcon Movement

It is difficult to understand, other than in personal terms and historical sentiment, why it was that the Folk put so much energy into reviving the SEI. One reason must be that Willi Hocke, a Sudeten (Czech) German and former SEI secretary, had escaped from the Nazis and was living in exile in Britain. He maintained contact with the Folk and was a close personal friend of Henry Fair (National Organiser) and Margaret White (later to become General Secretary). The Folk's pre-war contacts with SEI affiliates and the warm comradeship engendered by the international camps especially those of 1937 and 1939, was particularly poignant given the fascist destruction of the entire youth movement and the murder of so many of its finest daughters and sons.

It was as much a tribute to lost friends and a mark of international solidarity that motivated Fair, Rawson and Hocke to proceed with the work of reconstruction. However, although this might go some way to explain the choice of SEI/IFM, it does not account for the fact that, uncharacteristically, the Folk appeared to ignore a major development in the creation of another international youth organisation. This was the World Youth Conference which was held at the Royal Albert Hall in London in November 1945. The conference established the World Federation of Democratic Youth (WFDY), which until 1948, when the politics of the cold war began to bite, was the only truly international (as opposed to being solely based on Europe), non-sectarian youth organisation. There can be no doubt that this was a major event, the patrons of which were prominent politicians, artists and intellectuals from many countries spanning all continents.

Despite travel difficulties, delegates came from almost every country in the world and the conference received messages of support from the US President Truman, Attlee (British Prime Minister), Bevin (Foreign Secretary) and most of the major world[5] leaders. The British delegation consisted of representatives or observers from Jewish youth organisations, the National Union of Students, Young Conservatives, Young Liberals, youth councils from many different towns, various trade unions, the Church of England Youth Council, the BFYC and many others.[6] It is strange indeed the Folk was not counted among this number especially since the event was held in London. By 1948, the WFDY was regarded by western governments as pro-communist (largely because its affiliates were from socialist and non-socialist countries alike) and as a consequence the International Union of Youth and Students (IUSY) was hastily conceived in 1946 as 'a bulwark against communism in post-war Europe.'[7] As we shall see, this organisation, once it had solved its internal wrangles, was to develop strong links with the IFM. It is doubtful, however, whether the communist bogey would have deterred the Folk from the WFDY, but certainly it influenced the IFS/IFM - but by this time the die was cast and the Folk was committed to the IFM for better or worse.

Initially Woodcraft Folk was very highly regarded within the IFM given the important part it had played in its re-foundation. In recognition of this, Basil Rawson was the first president of the International Falcon Secretariat. It is noteworthy that the aspirant new international did not revert to its pre war name - Socialist Education International. This would have alienated the youth organisations in the Scandinavian countries. The Folk had no objection to the word 'socialist', but was wary of it in its party political sense. Hence when, in 1952, it was proposed that the International Falcon Secretariat (IFS) should affiliate to the Socialist International, the Folk opposed this arguing that:

> The IFS is concerned with children's work. Membership of a body co-ordinating adult work is not in accordance with our programme.[8]

However the Folk's prestigious status counted for little when the initial post war euphoria had died down and the grim reality of a world divided by an imaginary 'iron curtain' presented itself. The difficulties the Folk faced in the IFM were political. Put simply, in the context of the ensuing cold war, the IFM, until the later 1960s adopted a persistent anti-communist stance. The Folk, on the other hand, took literally the IFM motto 'Span the World With Friendship' and were thus unwilling to participate in or approve of anything which exacerbated tensions between east and west. Indeed, as we shall see, the Folk went further, and established its own relationships with children's organisations in socialist countries - an act of independence of which the IFM strongly disapproved.

The IFS made its anti-communism and its opposition to the WFDY evident early on. For example in a report on a UNESCO conference attended by a wide range of youth organisations, Henrik de Wijn (IFS secretary) wrote:

> Conference started in an atmosphere of mistrust and tension caused by the (usual) behaviour of the communist delegates, opposing everything and by wasting time with long explanations.[9]

It was in 1954, however, that the tension between the Folk and the IFM rose to the surface. In that year the Folk established contacts with children's organisations in Poland and the Soviet Union. Margaret White joined a delegation to the latter country and Dot Ballantine represented the Folk on a visit to Poland. Lorenz Knorr, the leader of the West German Falcons wrote to Henrik de Wijn drawing the attention of the IFM to these contacts and doubted whether 'the IFM can observe patiently when one organisation acts in any field of international understanding which cannot be approved by other organisations'. He went on to cast aspersions on the action of the Woodcraft Folk on the grounds that 'it includes in its membership a considerable number of communists.'[10] De Wijn, in circulating extracts from Knorr's letters announced that the issue would be discussed at the next meeting of the International Committee. A correspondence ensued, the details of which were summarised and circulated to affiliates by de Wijn.

In view of the seriousness of the matter and the Folk's role in it, it is worth examining the material in some detail. Sven Arne Stahre, the leader of the Swedish affiliate, Unge Ornar, wrote to de Wijn to say that his organisation saw nothing wrong with the Folk position. Many organisations in Sweden, including the Social Democratic Party had contacts with the Soviet Union and visited frequently. He acknowledged that other countries, for example West Germany, might view east/west links in a different light, but each country had the right to decide for itself and 'the fact that Woodcraft Folk may have a number of communist members'[11] should not alter the principle of autonomy. On behalf of the Folk, Margaret White replied to Knorr's charges thus:

> We challenge the statement that there are a number of communists in our organisation, but in any case, if there are, that does not make our organisation communist. We are broadly socialist and as such, wish to make contact with socialists all over the world. We want to make our motto a living thing and really 'Span the World with Friendship'. Our executive wish to express strong doubts about the attitude of Lorenz's letters and his international philosophy.[12]

This letter from the Folk prompted an extraordinarily partisan and hectoring response from de Wijn. He ticked off the Folk for its observation about Knorr and advised it to,

> ... consider the position of western Germany in respect with

(sic) Soviet Russia and it will at least understand that our German friends must be disappointed by the attitude of those organisations who do not seem to have objections against visits to communist countries ... (the) Netherlands organisation [de Wijn's] will never accept an invitation of this type and I can only hope that the International Committee of the IFM will adopt the same attitude.[13]

He went on to say that although he too wanted to 'span the world with friendship', he refused 'to visit a country like a sort of prisoner with secret agents on my heels'.

The cards were clearly stacked against the Folk and the result of its failure to capitulate to cold war ideology was that Basil Rawson was removed from the presidency of the IFM and although he accepted the fact graciously, National Folk Council was in no doubt that he was the victim of a political manoeuvre. Folk Council passed a resolution to be sent to de Wijn registering the Woodcraft Folk's 'formal protest against the election of a president without prior notice or opportunity for nominating being given to the individual member organisations' and, in obvious reference to the election of Anton Teserak as the incoming IFM president, the resolution added 'that all future presidents of the IFM shall be practising members of their organisation'.[14]

Undaunted, the Folk continued its links with children's organisations in the socialist countries with the result that it was even less happy with the IFM's anti-communism which surfaced unfailingly with each turn in the international situation. The crisis in Hungary in 1956 was a good case in point. The appearance of Soviet troops in Budapest prompted Henrik de Wijn to declare that the Hungarians were:

victims of the dirtiest Russian treason ... Stalin may be dead and blamed but the same develish (sic) spirit is still governing Russia and the poor countries put under its terrifying control.[15]

He went on to suggest menacingly that in the light of this, the International Committee would have to consider its attitude to affiliates who have contact with 'iron curtain countries'.[16] The Folk responded:

Whilst viewing with concern, from a humanitarian point of view, the tragic events in Hungary ... we object to the inferred threat to organisations making contact with children's organisations in other countries whether they are members of the IFM or not.[17]

De Wijn took strong objection to this letter since according to him 'one can find those words in the communist press' and hence he was 'not able to acknowledge the protest'. Things looked grim. However, Rawson's fear that the Folk would be expelled from the IFM did not materialise at this stage. It may be due to the fact that de Wijn had overstepped the mark given his own acknowledgment that it was not usual for the IFM to make political comments.

Despite Basil Rawson's desire to promote unity and his use of skilful diplomacy, it was clear that the cold war noose was tightening. The 7th IFM Conference in 1959 resolved that the only organisations eligible for IFM affiliated status were those 'recognised and recommended by a national organisation in its own country affiliated to the ICFTU[18], the International Federation of Workers' Education Associations, the Socialist International and the Asian Socialist Conference. This would have excluded all African countries and possibly the Folk itself had it not been already affiliated. In a deft move to circumvent this sectarianism Rawson added, with agreement, that where there were difficulties the judgment of individual affiliated organisations should be trusted.[19] However, this fancy footwork only managed to paper over the cracks. The early 1960s witnessed the Folk once again in the eye of the cold war storm.

In 1961 the German Democratic Republic (GDR) erected a wall to divide east and west Berlin. The whole of Berlin was situated geographically in the east, in the GDR, but the post second world war settlement had divided the city originally into four zones of occupation. By the late 1950s, the city was effectively divided in half - a pro-capitalist zone and pro-socialist one which was the capital of the GDR. The construction of the wall precipitated the predicable 'Berlin crisis' - predictable in the sense that Berlin was the focal point, in a literal sense, of the cold war division of Europe. Needless to say the IFM had made a strong statement attacking the GDR. Margaret White on behalf of Woodcraft Folk objected to this strongly partisan position and wrote a letter of protest[20] in which she expressed her organisation's concern about the situation in West Germany - in particular the fact that many former Nazis were in power there and that West German re-armament posed a threat to world peace. She added that the Folk opposed all nuclear weapons, whichever 'side' controlled them. In anticipation of opposition the letter ended;

> Woodcraft Folk has more than once been a lone voice within the IFM and some of our colleagues have behaved in a way

they try to reserve when talking of their political opponents.

De Wijn took great exception to this and retaliated by attempting to divide the Woodcraft Folk leadership. He wrote to Basil Rawson complaining about Margaret White's letter and saying that he would not reply to it until Rawson had given his views.[21] De Wijn was to be disappointed. Rawson, the respected elder statesman of the IFM, backed White all the way. He told de Wijn,[22] that despite the fact that she had raised some unrelated issues in her letter to him, its general line 'speaks for the British movement', not only for the Woodcraft Folk but 'also constituency parties of the LABOUR PARTY' [BR's capital letters]. Just in case there was any doubt as to where he stood, Rawson, cleverly turning the anti-communist argument on its head, went on to say:

> We are sometimes alarmed that adult members of the IFM in some cases forget that our work is international rather than partisan ... as socialists we cannot agree with the politics of the West German government.

But, he went on to say, this fact did not deter the Folk's desire to make links with children's organisations in West Germany.

Henrik de Wijn resigned as IFM secretary in 1962. One of the reasons he gave for his departure in a letter to Sven Arne Stahre (Tesarek's successor as IFM President) was 'the feeling that a number of organisations in the IFM, or at least certain leading personalities, are no longer ready to appreciate my conception of international work.'[23] It might be thought that this was a reference to Basil Rawson (as one of the 'leading personalities') with whom, as we have seen, de Wijn had frequent clashes over international issues. Indeed at the very meeting at which de Wijn announced his resignation a row had broken out on the International Committee following Rawson's objection to the use of the term 'iron curtain countries'. However, as Rawson's carefully preserved IFM papers show[24] de Wijn believed that he was the victim of behind-the-scenes manoeuvring orchestrated by the Austrians. Despite their political differences, de Wijn seemed to regard Rawson as his only ally. He wrote a 'confidential and personal' letter to Rawson[25] in which expressed the 'greatest concern' about the future of the IFM if the Austrian nominee, Kurt Biak, took over as the IFM secretary: Biak, according to de Wijn 'is no independent person but a servant of his bosses in Vienna. THEY will direct him.'[26] One can only speculate as to whom 'they' referred, but it is likely that this was a reference to the

91

Austrian Social Democratic party and the Second International. Certainly de Wijn's fears that smaller affiliates would be 'ruled out' by an Austrian takeover struck a chord with Rawson who expressed great regret at the 'shameful and inexcusable behaviour' suffered by de Wijn.

Despite the change in leadership, there was no change in the anti-communist politics of the IFM and disapproval of the Folk's independent line remained the order of the day. A huge row blew up when the Folk organised an International Seminar of leaders of children's and youth organisations in Coventry 6-11th April 1963. Representatives of youth organisations from 12 countries attended the seminar. Included amongst these were socialist countries. The seminar was welcomed by the Lord Mayor of Coventry and the local council 'afforded warm hospitality'.[27] The seminar was still under way when Kurt Biak wrote to Basil Rawson asking for an explanation and alleging that the Folk had broken IFM rules by inviting a communist organisation to attend from an IFM country - Finland. Furthermore the Folk was charged with hosting a meeting of the Executive Committee of CIMEA (the children's section of WFDY).[28] When these matters were reported to the International Committee of the IFM it pronounced that the Easter seminar of the Woodcraft Folk was 'a severe break of the Emergency resolution adopted at the 8th International Conference'[29] (Vienna 1962) and demanded a written declaration from the Folk that it would not repeat the same offence. This resolution banned contacts with communist organisations (or organisation 'sympathising' with communists) in countries where IFM or an IFM affiliate existed. Furthermore it forbade IFM affiliates from participating in 'gatherings arranged by international organisations within the communist sphere of influence'.[30]

Once again the threat of expulsion was in the air especially given that Folk's initial response clearly did not satisfy the IFM, although it was able to disprove the CIMEA charge and deflected the Finnish one, since the Folk had invited all IFM affiliates. Rawson once again provided a formula to prevent a breach. In an undated and unsigned report of the International Committee he recounted himself as having said that 'insofar as they regarded our action as a mistake we accepted that from their point of view we had made a mistake'. The Folk, however, refused to provide the written declaration the IFM required - the most it was prepared to do was to affirm that it did not have direct contact with non IFM children's organisations in IFM affiliated countries, and that its 'record of loyalty to the IFM bears inspection by any other member country'.[31] This was interpreted by the International Committee of the IFM as an acceptance by the Folk of the standpoint of the IFM.[32] The dispute eventually wore itself out but not before Biak had raised the inevitable charge of communist infiltration in the Woodcraft Folk - a 'fact' which he claimed had been raised with him by IRIS, the anti-communist trade union journal. Clearly this smear campaign had some effect at 'grass roots' level. In a circular to Folk Council members[33], Margaret White suggested that an official protest be made to the IFM regarding the 'ugly incidents' a Woodcraft Folk delegation to Denmark endured at the hands of the West German Falcons because the latter objected to the fact that some Folk members wore a badge from the GDR.

'Ostpolitik' and the IFM

Although the policy of détente on an international level did not get under way until the 1970s, there was, nonetheless a sign of a moderate thaw in the unrelenting cold war during the 1960s. In 1962-3 Willi Brandt, (then leader of the German Social Democrat Party, mayor of West Berlin and later, Foreign Minister and then Chancellor of West Germany) developed his party's policy of 'ostpolitik' (eastern policy). This was a pragmatic policy based on the fact that West Germany was in a strategically vulnerable position, situated as she was, on the 'fault line' of east west conflict in Europe. Given this Brandt argued that unless Germans desired perpetual conflict, the only way forward was to recognise the post-war division of Europe, and in the case of West Germany to accept the existence of the GDR. The Warsaw Pact countries were very receptive to such overtures and this is why modern historians have regarded 'ostpolitik' as a precursor to détente.[34] But although détente had to wait for another decade, it is clear that Brandt's policy had an impact in social democratic circles, and in particular in the Socialist International. This in turn influenced the thinking of the Socialist Youth International and hence of the IFM.

Within the IFM the Folk's own 'ost-politik' now won an important new ally in the form of the West German Falcon organisation. Given that the latter had been so vehemently anti-communist during the 1950s and that it was one of the largest IFM affiliates, its change of policy was particularly significant. It explains why Lorenz Knorr, on behalf of German Falcons attended the Woodcraft Folk seminar in Coventry in 1963. In 1966, Brodo Brucher, the German Falcon's representative on the IFM International Committee, explained that his organisation wanted 'not ideological fraternisation but a dialogue'[35] and that although this dialogue had suffered a reverse at the end of the 1950s, it had been renewed in 1962 with their first contact with the Soviet Union.

Contacts and exchanges had been made with Czechoslovakia and, he reported, discussion was under way respecting contacts with the GDR.

However, it was not until 1967 that the IFM, despite the occasional mildly positive signal, finally dropped its ban on contacts with socialist countries. To some extent the way had already been prepared for this by International Leaders' Conference on *The Future Work of the IFM* 1966. This was a wide ranging discussion reviewing the IFM's work as a predominantly European organisation, and preparing the way for changes which would make it more genuinely international and would give it a more accessible identity. Clearly east-west contact was an inevitable part of the discussion. Biak outlined the present IFM policy. The Woodcraft Folk view that the IFM policy should be reviewed was, this time, supported by the French and the West Germans. However, although it was decided to compile information on the existing east-west contacts of affiliates and to look at the possibility of a joint conference between IFM and non-IFM members, it was clear that opponents of this line were strong enough to negate this by insisting that if the IFM was to look at links with communist organisations then it should do the same with fascist ones. On behalf of Woodcraft Folk, Jack Colbert argued that a distinction must be made between communist and fascist countries and that nothing should be done to 'jeopardise the underground socialist liberation in these (fascist) countries.[36]

An extraordinary IFM conference was held in 1967 to approve a rule change which would enable the IFM to appoint a full-time general secretary and employ an independent secretariat. Miguel Martinez was appointed as the first full-time IFM general secretary. He was also vice president of the IUSY and retained this post.[37] This decision had financial implications which clearly had a bearing on IFM's ever more insistent appeal for additional revenue. This was another issue on which the Folk had cause for argument with the IFM, since it was one of the smaller and poorer affiliates, and one which, unlike most of the others, received no financial support from a socialist party. The issue came to head over the IFM's decision to transfer the burden of travel costs for attendance at meetings of the International Committee on to those affiliates holding a seat. The Folk bitterly complained that this was 'a negation of democracy',[38] since poorer affiliates would be prevented from standing for election if their organisations could not afford their fares during their 3 year period of office. Martinez was obdurately unsympathetic to the Folk's plight. Of more significance was the fact that at this conference a resolution was passed in which IFM affiliates were urged 'to take up contacts and invite a dialogue with the official bodies of the communist children and youth organisations'.[39] At last, it would seem, the anti-cold war position of the Folk had triumphed.

1968

The victory at the 1967 conference was a pyrrhic one, since the Soviet invasion of Czechoslovakia in 1968, gave the cold warriors a new lease of life. The 10th IFM International Conference in 1968 adopted a resolution which, whilst condemning the Warsaw Pact occupation and regarding it as 'a hard set-back against all those who have worked for peace and relaxation of tension',[40] nonetheless called for an intensification of east/west contacts. However, at the same time, the conference re-iterated its policy adopted at the 1962 International Conference (Vienna) which prohibited co-operation between IFM affiliates and any other international organisations. According to one of the Woodcraft Folk delegates 'the whole conference was a concerted political attack on E.W. exchanges.'[41] In contrast, National Folk Council deplored events in Czechoslovakia, but at the same time was aware that 'this would give rise to a new era in the Cold War' and hence was determined to intensify its international contacts. A letter was sent to Czechoslovakia along these lines.[42] More controversially the Folk sent a delegation to the 9th World Youth Festival in Sofia, Bulgaria, organised by the WFDY - an event officially boycotted by the IFM.

Clearly the tension between the IFM and its recalcitrant British affiliate was mounting in 1968, particularly in view of the fact that the Folk was embroiled in conflict with the IFM leadership on a series of other matters like the organisation and timing of international camps, finance and other issues. In general the Folk was outmanouvred and isolated in these disputes - a fact which was clearly connected with an attempt to marginalise the Folk's political line and which led ultimately to its loss of its place on the International Committee when Basil Rawson retired from it in 1968.

Two of the Folk's delegates to the 1968 IFM Conference, Peggy Aprahamian and Tony Raine submitted damning reports to National Folk Council of the conference itself and the politics of the IFM generally. The former was a withering political critique of the anti-communist social democratic politics of the IFM, whilst the latter was a highly critical attack on the organisational inefficiency of the International. Whether intentional or not the two reports complemented each other. Tony Raine had been designated as Rawson's successor on the International Committee, but because of the extreme unease about the politics of the conference, the Folk delegation decided that he should not stand as a mark of protest and that it would be easier to fight what the Folk now regarded as a reactionary leadership if one was not part of it. The Germans thought and acted in the same way. However, at the last minute Raine changed his mind, entered his name on the ballot and received a derisory vote. The Folk's continued membership of the IFM was now seriously questioned. It is thus richly ironical that the closest the Folk came to disaffiliating from the IFM coincided with the moment when the policy for which it had been fighting in respect of east/west contacts was, in formal terms, making great, albeit halting, progress. In order to understand why it was that after 22 years of patient albeit critical work with the IFM, the Folk now adopted more militant tactics, one must look at Raine and Aprahamian's report in more detail.

The IFM and Social Democratic Politics

The essence of Aprahamian's critique of the IFM was that the IFM was a very small body covering only a minority of children's organisations and that it was dominated by right wing social democrats 'concerned to fulfil their historical role of stemming the tide of militant socialism and propping up capitalist Europe'.[43] In her view the IFM tolerated internal opposition (ie from Britain and West Germany) only because this came from two important NATO countries and the right wing caucus was strong enough to withstand it especially since they were busy bolstering their control by drawing on new sources of support from 'hand picked' organisations outside Europe and in the developing countries. Hence she was pessimistic about any possibility of progressive change and for this reason she judged that the IFM leadership 'can afford to go through the motions of debate against the fine facade of democracy without any fear of defeat.'[44] Whilst not explicitly criticising Basil Rawson's tactics of compromise and diplomacy in an effort to pursue a progressive agenda within the IFM, Peggy Aprahamian now questioned whether it would be wise to continue such a course - as she put it: 'we should not necessarily assume that because we were a party to its foundation that we should necessarily remain in its fold'. Tony Raine did not go as far as suggesting disaffiliation, but expressed himself 'rather pleased that we are no longer committed to alien policies simply because we are a committee member'. His view was that the Folk had gone far enough and that it should now 'begin a campaign within the IFM to bring individual affiliated organisations round to our way of thinking'. He was appalled by the 'behind-the scenes horse-trading' and concluded that the conference was 'obviously suited more to the talents of life-long politicians than a children's educator of socialist principles'.[45]

How valid were these criticisms or were they just the outraged reaction of naive newcomers to the rough and tumble of the international scene? Why should these Woodcraft Folk delegates, (particularly Aprahamian), be so shocked by the political stance of the IFM when it was obvious that it had been anti-communist since its inception? In part the explanation lies in the increasing lack of independence of the IFM and its growing subordination to the day-to-day political interests of its social democratic paymasters - a process which began in 1962 when the organisation's headquarters were transferred to Vienna. A good example of this can be found when, contrary to the recommendations of the Leaders' Conference of 1967, the Salzburg planning meeting for the 1968 International Camp scheduled to be held in Dobriach, Austria, failed to discuss the inclusion of children's organisations from the socialist countries. According to Gill Gilpin, the Woodcraft Folk representative at the Salzburg meeting, the reason for this was that the Austrian Social Democratic Party had suffered setbacks in recent elections and its leaders feared the worst '... if they lend themselves to anything so revolutionary as exchanges between children of the east and the west'.[46] Miguel Martinez, elected as IFM general secretary in 1967, had ambitious plans for the IFM as a major player within the Socialist International (SI). Shortly after taking up his new post Martinez announced that the IFM would 'participate in all major Socialist International events in order to appear publicly in the international field ... and in order to meet democratic socialist political leaders.'[47] Evidently the SI did not respond with the enthusiasm which Martinez had anticipated. As a result he wrote to all of the leaders of the European Socialist and Labour Parties explaining his plans for the IFM. The following is an extract from a letter he sent to the British Labour Party:

> ... since I was elected Secretary General ... it has been my intention to get into very close co-operation with the different international organisations of the Labour Movement. In the last few months, I have been able to realise that because of its educational and social character, the IFM may become a fairly important and respected international body. But I was elected Secretary General as a socialist and this is why I want definitely to develop the IFM as part of the socialist world. This is the basic reason ... for ... getting in close contact with ... the Socialist International. Unfortunately, the response ... [has] been most disappointing ... the SI will consider the

participation of the IFM ... in the matters directly concerning our movement or in matters where it is believed we can make a contribution.[48]

Martinez considered the SI response to be an insulting rebuff, and hoped that the Labour Party as an SI affiliate would help the IFM cause. He declared in the same letter:

I am really shocked to see that the SI refuses to treat the IFM as a fraternal organisation ....we can hardly explain the reason for it ... Despite the negative and impolite response of the SI, I will keep on trying to project internationally such a reality.

Despite Martinez's political ambitions and the setback of the 1968 conference, the Folk claimed that its decision not to disaffiliate from the IFM had been vindicated. At the IFM Conference of 1970 in Dusseldorf the Folk was re-elected onto the International Committee. (Margaret White and Tony Raine shared the seat). Visitors from Hungary, Roumania and Yugoslavia attended the conference and the Folk was welcomed back to the fold. Its work was praised: 'Thanks to its ever important contacts with the Co-operative movement ... our friends are becoming one of the most active youth organisations in Great Britain.'[49] What had changed? The key factor was the election of a social democratic government in West Germany headed by Willi Brandt pursuing détente policies, which meant that, according to Tony Raine 'it was now more respectable to pursue east/west contacts'. Those very same IFM affiliates who, because they did 'not enjoy ... [the Folk's] ... independence of outlook and ... [had]... to defer to their adult political bodies',[50] proclaimed the cold war message so stridently in 1968, now two years later reversed their position. Although the Folk had done a great deal to prepare the ground for this, it would be naïve to presume that its stand, brave and principled as it was over many years, had been solely responsible for the change in the IFM. Cold war politics and its interface with social democratic pragmatism had an internal dynamic of its own. However, it can be said with some justification, that once the IFM policy changed, the rapidity with which it could be put into effect was greatly assisted by the Folk's years of experience in conducting east/west exchanges. By 1971 the Folk was able to say that it was 'excited by the development of the IFM' and 'the pathway we pioneered is being trod by thousands'[51], although in 1973 it voluntarily relinquished its position on the International Committee for 'financial reasons'. The final stage in reversing the cold war policy was taken in

1976 when, after many abortive attempts, an official seminar on educational work among children was organised jointly by the IFM and its 'communist' counterpart, CIMEA (Comite International des Mouvements d'Enfants et d'Adolescents).

The Folk established its own relationship with CIMEA, despite the fact that in 1985, the National Secretary was at pains to point out that the Folk was a 'corresponding' organisation and as such had no formal status. The CIMEA General Secretary, Sandor Molnari, had apparently considered the Folk as having 'observer category' of membership. Despite its anomalous status, the Folk undoubtedly made good use of its CIMEA link. At a conference on peace education organised by CIMEA in Potsdam in 1980, the Folk made new contacts with children's organisations in the Caribbean, Africa & Asia. Financial considerations determined the Folk's relationship with the IFM from 1973 onwards. The fact that the Folk relinquished its full membership in 1980 and assumed associate status, was not due to political differences - this phase was now over, although an undated document[52] not only raises the question of the huge budget deficit of the IFM but attributed this to the fact that money is:

> squandered attending non-productive meetings, jetting around the world and not dealing with fundamental problems. Problems like the complete demise of Falcon groups in Holland, the isolation of the Swiss Falcons and the ability of some member organisations to promote international exchanges ...

It was mot until 1998 that the Folk once again became a full member of the IFM. The demise of the socialist countries between 1989-1999 meant, of course, that CIMEA ceased to exist.

Woodcraft Folk's international work

The question remains, however, why did the Folk take the stand it did in its international work and what, if any, results did it yield, apart from 20 years of conflict within the IFM? Clearly, given the nature of the IFM politics, the Folk's determination to pursue a 'go it alone' policy of détente at the height of the cold war is something of a paradox. This is especially puzzling given that, contrary to what its detractors would have wished, the leadership of the Folk was not a sinister band of communists. The authors or early champions of its international policy were all Labour Party members: Basil Rawson,

Margaret White, Dot Ballantine et al. Yet the course they embarked upon in 1954 with the first visits to the socialist countries (USSR and Poland) incurred the ire of all but communists and those who remained open-minded enough not to be taken in by the red scare climate. For in this respect the judgement of the Folk was prescient indeed. There is little indication that the 1950s generation in Britain which had such admiration for the war-time record of its former ally, the Soviet Union, would be won round to the opposite view quite so quickly. We have no record of the thinking behind the Folk's policy; but certainly it would not appear that they were out of touch with the thinking of 'ordinary people'. The membership although stagnant in the 1950s, grew steadily in the 1960s and 1970s and whilst this cannot be attributed to the Folk's international policy, the fact is that the policy did not harm the organisation. The exchanges with socialist countries flourished and were undoubtedly very popular, at least until 1978 when the Annual Report recorded a falling off in their number. The reason given for this was prohibitive costs and the fact 'leaders are no longer so excited to plan for long journeys across Europe when adventurous and exciting holidays can be planned in Britain'. The 1986 World Youth Festival was held in Moscow. Despite the fact that the Foreign Office warned against it, characterising such festivals as 'thinly disguised instruments of Soviet foreign policy', the British Youth Council (BYC) decided to participate, although the Folk did not on the grounds that the event catered for the over 16 age group. The Folk sent a small delgation as part of the the BYC contingent.

During the Cold War the Folk's international work was pioneering. By the 1980s, when the notion of peace and detente was more widely accepted and foreign travel began to lose its allure as it became more affordable and widespread, the Folk's international work was no longer unique. What remains, however, are the International Camps held every 4-5 years. These still flourish and are enormously popular as 2-4,000 children and young people from many countries and every continent gather under canvass in the English countryside, grouped in 'villages' and live communally and in harmony for 2 weeks.

Notes

1   There is very little available in English: Two out of print booklets exist in (bad) translation: *70 Years Socialistic Youth International*, H Eppe & W Ullenberg, German Falcons, Bonn 1977. This is an overview of all the European non-communist internationals which includes a section on the SEI/IFM. *The Falcon Organisations in East and Central Europe from 1923 until now*, H Eppe & O Lambert, IFM-SEI nd (Deals with individual

countries) In addition a book, *The History of the International Socialist Youth Movement*, L Radomir, Leyden, Sijthoff 1970, concentrates on youth and students.

2   Eppe & Ullenberg, op cit, p30. The Comintern, or Third (Communist) International, was established by the Bolsheviks after the revolution. Its 21 Theses drafted by Lenin and adopted in 1921 were specifically framed to exclude non-revolutionary parties.

3   *Angry Young Man* op cit, p257

4   *Early Days* op cit, p37

5   Another organisation, the World Assembly of Youth (WAY) was established in 1948 as a pro-capitalist alternative.

6   See *Forward for our Future!* Official report of the World Youth Conference, WFDY 1945

7   Eppe & Ullenberg, op cit, p81

8   *Falcons' Outlook* no.1 1952, YMA/WF/338/9

9   *Falcons' Outlook* no.2 February 1952, YMA/WF/338/9

10   Circular letter from Henrik de Wijn to members of the IFM International Committee, 8/12/1954, YMA/WF/156

11   Circular letter from Henrik de Wijn to members of the IFM International Committee, 25/1/1955, YMA/WF/156

12   Ibid

13   Ibid

14   National Folk Council Minutes, 14/15th May 1955, WF archive

15   *Falcons' Outlook*, 'Shocking news from Hungary' H de Wijn, vol.v no.11 November 1956, YMA/WF/338-9

16   Ibid

17   Margaret White to Henrik de Wijn, *Falcons' Outlook*, vol.v no.12 December 1956

18   The International Confederation of Free Trade Unions (ICFTU) was the American-backed rival to the World Federation of Trade Unions (WFTU). The latter was founded in 1945 and the former 3 years later.

19   Report of 7th IFM International Conference, 1-3 April 1959, YMA/WF/161

20   Margaret White to de Wijn 18th October 1961, YMA/WF/163

21   De Wijn to Rawson 12th November 1961, ibid

22   Rawson to de Wijn 27th December 1961, ibid

23   *Falcons' Outlook* vol.XI, no.1 April 1962

24   It should be noted that this appears to be the only record of the WF's international work. Minutes of WF's own international committee seem to have been mislaid. Thankfully Rawson's IFM collection is in the archive at BLEPS, along with a full set of *Falcons' Outlook*.

25   De Wijn to Rawson, 18th February 1962 YMA/WF/164

26   Ibid

27   1963 Annual report of the Woodcraft Folk, expanded section on *International Work*, p8. Folk House archive

28   Biak to Rawson, 9th April 1963, YMA/WF/165

29   IFM circular 25th April 1963, ibid

101

30 Report of 8th IFM International Conference, 1962, YMA/WF/164
31 Letter from M.White, T.Hawkes and B.Rawson to K.Biak 15th July 1864, YMA/WF/166
32 IFM International Committee minutes, 2nd June 1964, ibid
33 21st August 1963, ibid
34 See for example: T E Vadney *The World Since 1945*, Penguin 1992. S Padgett & W E Paterson *A History of Social Democracy in Postwar Europe*, Longman 1991
35 Report on International Leaders' Conference on *The Future Work of the IFM* 1966, p10 YMA/WF/168
36 Ibid p12
37 He had, until 1967, been employed by IUSY as Assistant General Secretary.
38 M White to Miguel Martinez (new IFM General Secretary), 30th October 1967, YMA/WF/169
39 *Falcon's Outlook*, no.3 1967, YMA/WF/339
40 *IFM*, Nov-Dec 1968 YMA/WF/339
41 Peggy Aprahamian's report to National Folk Council on IFM International Conference, Vienna 1968, YMA/WF/170
42 Woodcraft Folk Annual Report 1968, WF archive
43 P Aprahamian, op cit
44 Ibid
45 T Raine, report to National Folk Council on IFM International Conference, Vienna 1968, YMA/WF/170
46 Gill Gilpin's report to NFC on 'visit to Salzburg 20-30th September 1967', YMA/WF/169
47 IFM circular 28th November 1967, YMA/WF/169
48 Letter from Martinez to Gwn Morgan. Quoted by Margaret White in a circular to NFC, 21st September 1967, ibid
49 *IFM* 6/70, YMA/WF/340
50 T Raine, Report to NFC on 1970 IFM Special Conference, YMA/WF/172
51 *Woodcraft Folk Leaders Manual*, 1971, WF
52 The International Exchanges and contacts of the Woodcraft Folk

Chapter 8

THE FOLK AFTER THE SECOND WORLD WAR

It was only after the second world war that the kind of changes in the Woodcraft Folk that Leslie Paul and Joseph Reeves had advocated in 1934/5 were once again contemplated, albeit for different reasons and in different circumstances. Like most voluntary organisations the Folk emerged considerably weaker after the war. Its membership had halved by 1940 (to 2,558) and although it had begun to rise by 1946 (2,892), it was still nowhere near its 1939 figure of 5,134. The war had interrupted what might otherwise have been a period of expansion. By 1939 Henry Fair had been appointed to the first full-time post in the Folk's history - that of National Organiser and, in addition the Folk had established its own premises and headquarters at 13 Ritherdon Road, Tooting, London. Fair, however, was one of the few who recognised that if the Folk was to survive after the war it would need to establish a less confusing identity for itself. It is unclear whether his 1943 proposals[1] were given serious discussion - most of them were not implemented except those relating to the Labour Party and the TUC (see chapter 6). The proposals were very radical. Fair believed that the name "Woodcraft Folk" was not understood and should eventually be dropped. Meanwhile he suggested that the organisation should call itself the Woodcraft Folk Red Falcons or the Woodcraft Folk Co-operative/ Socialist Pioneers. The fringed jerkin should be dropped in favour of a simpler Folk costume along the lines of the Red Falcon uniform worn in most continental European countries. In addition he thought that Folk names for individuals and all arcane terminology should be disused since these 'waste time and cause confusion'. Most radical of all was the suggestion that the educational work of the Folk needed a thorough revision, in particular he had 'the impression that much of our 'red indianism' does not appeal now'.

However, the success of the 1946 International Camp in Brighton must have encouraged those who were opposed to such far-reaching changes and who thus assumed that the Folk would be able to pick up where it had left off before the war. The plan for the Folk's future development adopted in 1946[2] was wildly optimistic. It was agreed that by 1947 the Folk would double its membership, obtain premises in central London, appoint an additional full-time worker and develop outside contacts by taking advantage of the Ministry of Education's

Youth Policy (see below). By 1949 it was clear that this 'minimum plan' of 1946 had failed and hence the 1949 internal investigation to examine the causes of the Folk's stagnation was established. The changes arising from this were not as far-reaching as those which had been proposed by Fair seven years earlier, and even those which were adopted secured only a narrow majority at the 1950 Annual Delegate Conference. The six page report presented to the 1950 ADC resulted in the abolition of Folk names for formal purposes. This had the immediate effect of ensuring that Folk documents like minutes of meetings, were comprehensible to the unitiated member and non-member alike. For example Basil Rawson was no longer referred to in writing as 'Brown Eagle', or Henry Fair as 'Koodoo'. Folk names were still used (and persist even now in some districts). One of the original reasons for their widespread use was that it established greater equality between children and leaders at a time when it was not socially acceptable for children to address adults by their first names. Many older Folk members continued to mourn the loss of this tradition. Sidney Pool (Hawkmoth), who had joined the Folk in 1927 and was the editor of *The Pioneer*, gave another explanation, many years later, for the use of Folk names - he said that they were used because 'they emphasised the break from everyday life and helped us to assume another identity'.[3] The most significant change was that which related to the Charter and Creed (see chapter 5).

Apart from the important contribution made by the Folk on the international scene (see chapter 8), the 1950s was, in general a period of stagnation the roots of which were not addressed by the limited changes made in 1950. Membership rose only slightly and financial problems were such that Fred Kempton who was appointed full-time General Secretary in 1947 had to relinquish his post a year later and Henry Fair was forced to resign as full-time National Organiser in 1954. Their replacement was a part-time General Secretary, Margaret White who was appointed in 1954. (She became full-time in 1969). Basil Rawson remained in his lay position as Headman. The rupture with the co-operative movement had deprived the Folk of its only source of regular external funding, but although the Folk's financial situation was dire, this was not presented as the only reason for its stagnation in the 1950s. The Annual Report of 1959 identified the 'you've never had it so good mentality' of the Macmillan Tory Government years as being responsible for the fact that 'so many people are not interested in making their contribution to the welfare of mankind'. This was a somewhat pessimistic over-statement given that by 1960 the Folk's membership showed an increase for the first time in many years.

Nonetheless it was a theme that re-emerged in the early 1960s when despite the growth of CND and the mass appeal of the Aldermaston marches, the Folk was still of the opinion that 'the pseudo affluence of our time encourages false values in the minds of young people and our task of educating for social change becomes more difficult and more necessary'. It was not enough to inculcate charitable and humanitarian attitudes: 'whilst encouraging our members to play their full part in such campaigns as the Freedom from Hunger Campaign - the important job is to educate them so that when they progress to adult social work, they work to change the society that allows the larger part of the world to be hungry'.[4] Nonetheless, membership continued to rise. This may be due to the fact that the 1961 ADC approved plans for establishing a teenage membership category - the Venturers and it was precisely this age group which was most attracted to the peace movement and the Folk's long standing support for it.

Despite the changes in the Folk and the development of a very recognisable youth culture in the 1960s, camping remained a central feature of Woodcraft Folk activity. The reason for this was explained in some detail at an IFM International Helper course[5] run by the Woodcraft Folk in 1964 in Coventry on the theme 'International Camp Work'. Basil Rawson gave the opening lecture in which he used the work of Engels to justify the practice of camping in modern society when it was clearly no longer the necessity it had been in primitive communities. Such primitive communities were, he said (quoting Engels)[6] 'socialistic in character'. Although earlier forms of Woodcraft had tended, according to Rawson, to be escapist, the Folk saw camping as 'an important and vital part' of Woodcraft's 'socialist educational method'[7]. He gave three reasons for this. The first was that camping had obvious physical benefits. The second was what he termed the 'value of influence of the environment' by which he meant that it was beneficial to escape the drabness of the city. The third value he attached to camping was regarded as the most important - the 'sharing in the government' of the camp which entailed a practical exercise in the operation of democracy. Camping thus reproduces 'socialist communities in which our children learn by experience and practice a better and truer way of living.' Rawson concluded by arguing that 'a child who repeatedly practices a socialist way of life as a member of a community at camp develops the habits which it eventually tends to apply ... everywhere in that other life, away from camp ... **we must use camping as the reproduction of socialist communities in which our children learn by experience and practice a better and truer way of living.**' (BR's emphasis). In the discussion that followed it was clear

105

that others did not share the Folk's 'purist' view of camping. The West German Falcons did not think it was necessary to 'go back to a primitive way of life ... we must master modern ways of life ... by going back to primitive ways we are building barriers against modern society'. It is interesting to note that during the course of this discussion, Rawson revealed in answer to a direct question on recapitulation theory that although 'more weight' was given to it before the war, 'he thought that there was quite a lot to commend the recapitulation idea'. Whilst recapitulation theory no longer underpins Woodcraft practice today, the Folk has, nonetheless, remained unshakeable in its commitment to camping. Almost 20 years later an article in a Woodcraft Folk magazine for parents and leaders, commended camping as a practical exercise in democracy in which 'all aspects of work and play can be harnessed to show the benefits of co-operation rather than confrontation or competition'.[8]

Camping thus stood the test of time. It was an activity shared by all Folk members and one which brought different districts together. However, as divisions became apparent in the Folk, camping and camping standards became a source of tension and unease as was demonstrated by the furore surrounding the 1981 Venturer camp. The row was about the observance of traditional camping practices and customs which included the wearing of Folk costume, the daily tidiness of the children and their tents and personal property (known as Wapenshaw) and camp democracy. Some of the districts at the camp enthusiastically camped in the time-honoured fashion, while others did not and regarded the traditions and practices as oppressive and authoritarian resulting, inevitably, in a clash of values. This in itself reflected in microcosm the clash between the newer recruits and the 'old guard' at a national level. Having received wildly conflicting reports from the districts involved who had grouped themselves into 'pro' and 'contra' factions, National Council conducted an enquiry into the camp. The recommendations[9] it made were noteworthy and related to the future development of the Folk (see below). In addition to camping under canvas, the outdoor ideal was facilitated by the opening of two centres for outdoor activities - one in the north of England, Lockerbrook near Sheffield which was opened in 1964 and, ten years later the Cudham activity centre in Kent, in the south of England.

In spite of Woodcraft Folk's financial difficulties and the consequent reduction in staffing, Margaret White achieved an enormous amount during her 30 years as General Secretary. The Folk's membership quadrupled (from approximately 4,000 to 16,000) during her tenure of office and this was despite the cold war climate and the 'red scare' stories about the Folk which were exacerbated by the Folk's brave international policy. So why was it that the Folk grew in the 1960s, developed rapidly in the 1970s and continued a steady growth in the 1980s? Among factors which can be identified are: the development of the youth service and the Folk's association with it, the demise of the co-operative movement's attempts at organising youth and the growth of the peace movement in the 1960s and then again in the 1980s. The first two factors were important in ensuring that the Folk had a sounder financial base which then enabled it to both harness and expand the gains in membership fostered by a strong peace movement. However, as we shall see, this expansion led to internal problems within the Folk as it struggled to find a new identity which would enable it both to consolidate the gains it had made as well as continuing to grow.

The Co-op

In 1960 the British Federation of Co-operative Youth which had been limping along unsuccessfully for some years, was finally wound up. In 1969 the same fate met the Co-operative Youth Movement. However the failure of the co-operative movement's own youth organisation did not, as the Folk would have wished, result in a significant membership boost for the latter despite the ADC resolution of 1969 which called for the integration of CYM into the Folk 'subject to the recognition of the WF as the national co-operative children's organisation, and supporting financial assistance'. The Woodcraft Folk's Annual Report for 1970 announced that it had not, as anticipated, benefited from CYM transfers. The main gain was a financial one. In 1961 the annual grant from the co-op was increased to £450. By 1973 the Education Executive of the Co-operative Union agreed that this should be raised to £1,500 for 5 years. When this was reviewed in 1978 by the full Education Committee the Folk asked for the grant to be raised to £3,500, but in the 'less friendly atmosphere'[10] the Folk were awarded £2,500.

In 1981 the General Secretary reported that the grant was likely to be cut owing to the financial difficulties of the co-op. In addition the Woodcraft Folk groups might have to find alternative accommodation for their weekly meetings since many co-op halls were faced with closure.[11] Given that the retrenchment of the co-op in the 1970s is a matter fact, it is hard to understand why Doug Bourn, who replaced Margaret White in 1984, chose to criticise his predecessor on the issue of the Folk's relationship with the co-op. In 1985 Bourn claimed that Woodcraft Folk was now 'flavour of the month' with the co-op and 'that if we had started to act a few years ago nationally with the movement in the way that I have in recent months, the rewards we are now getting may not have come as such a surprise to some people.'[12]

The Youth Service

Margaret White was alert to and participated in the opportunities provided by the creation of the Youth Service. In fact by 1978 she noted that some members felt that she was involved in too many Youth Service activities.[13] The history of state intervention in the youth service dates from 1939 with the Board of Education Circular 1486, *The Service of Youth*. Under its provisions a National Youth Committee was established under the aegis of the Ministry of Education and Local Education Authorities were urged to establish local youth committees. However, notwithstanding the significance of state involvement it what was previously a sector entirely predicated upon the voluntary principle, it was clear 20 years later, as the 1960 Albermarle Report, *The Youth Service in England and Wales* showed, that youth provision was totally inadequate. According to Bernard Davies, by the time this report was published, 'state interest [in the youth service] had all but evaporated'[14].

His view is that this was because the post-war social democratic interventionist approach to youth work was increasingly at odds with the practical realities of later Tory and Labour governments whose main concern was to cut public spending and thus regarded a state-funded youth service, which had survived for a century on philanthropy and voluntaryism, as increasingly unimportant. Nonetheless, according to the Youth Service Development Council (a body established by Albermarle), the Youth Service expanded during the 1960s, albeit not in the manner nor as quickly as its champions advocated.[15] However, the almost two decades of unbroken Tory government following their 1979 general election victory ushered in a new phase in the atrophy of the youth service.

The liberal ideals underpinning youth work were increasingly at variance with the Thatcherite attitude to working class youth. This was motivated by the desire to contain, readjust and re-moralise them into an acceptance of their social exclusion in the face of mass youth unemployment. It entailed the introduction of very different kind of youth initiatives in the form of the infamous and ill-fated Youth Opportunities Programme of 1978 and the Youth Training programme of 1981. Such schemes were in marked contrast to the ideas underpinning the creation of the Youth Service in the 1940s which, given the prevalence (until the late 1960s) of a juvenile labour shortage, viewed youth as a national asset.[16] This meant that the type of well funded inclusive youth service with purpose built accommodation and increased number of youth workers advocated by the Albermarle Committee (of which Leslie Paul was a member), was never really implemented since it was much cheaper to give grant aid to the existing voluntary youth organisations. However even this was greatly reduced by the 1980s due to massive government spending cuts and enforced (via 'rate capping' and other measures) reductions in local authority budgets.

Despite the fact that Woodcraft Folk was a voluntary organisation it consistently championed the cause of the state youth service. It had a full discussion on the Albermarle Report and campaigned for its implementation. By the early 1960s local districts of the Folk were beginning to become involved in their local youth committees. The 1966 ADC attempted to speed the process up. It called on all Woodcraft Folk organisations to register with their Local Education Authority's youth committee and the local Standing Conference of the Voluntary Youth Organisation (SCVYO) since this 'will ensure our participation in the advantages accruing from the operation of the Youth Service provisions in the Board of Education circular 1486 and also youth projects of social value arising from the implementation of the Newsom Report.' One of the conditions for receiving local funding was the non political status of the applicant organisation. Hence it is no accident that the same ADC also resolved to remind local leaders who were members of political parties to exercise care 'to prevent their enthusiasm for their political party overshadowing their responsibility to the Woodcraft Folk'.

Such warnings did not prevent an unprecedented attack by the Conservative Party on the Woodcraft Folk in 1975. The following circular was sent from Tory central office to all constituency agents:

> You may receive enquiries about the activities of the Woodcraft Folk, a group which is showing signs of increasing activity in some parts of the country and which has recently made applications for grants to Labour controlled councils ... The group which has some 13,000 members, has close links with the Co-operative Union and one of its political aims has been described as a Co-operative Commonwealth. The group promotes International Camps and arranges for overseas visits by members. Last year for instance, a delegation visited Poland as guests of the Supreme Co-operative Council.

Recommended talks to the children have included such titles as 'Karl Marx and the Working Men's International' and recommended songs to be taught have included 'Red Army March' and the 'Internationale'.

I shall be grateful if you will keep me informed of any activities of this group in your constituency and let me know of any application for financial assistance which may be made by the Woodcraft Folk.[17]

This precipitated a great flurry of national and local media interest in the Folk, most of it salacious. The *News of the World* unsurprisingly picked up the story[18] and reported that Conservative Central Office's main concern was about 'unrevealed amounts of ratepayers' money granted to the Woodcraft Folk by local authorities'. The smear campaign continued in 1976 - Margaret White appeared on the prime-time television news programme *Nationwide* to present the Woodcraft Folk case. The general view within the Folk was that the campaign backfired against Woodcraft Folk's detractors and that the issue served to rally support behind the beleaguered organisation. Some of the support was influential. The Lord Mayor and Lady Mayoress of Sheffield Council, Albert and Elsie Richardson (well known by their Folk names, Redwing and Heather) were Folk members. The as yet little known Sheffield Councillor, David Blunkett wrote a letter to the *Guardian* condemning the Tory campaign. The National Council of Voluntary Youth Service (NCVYS) also lent its support to the Folk over this issue.

Thus whilst it was true that the Tory attack served to place the Folk in the public eye and to demonstrate its lack of isolation, it nonetheless remained the case that some Tory local authorities continued to harry the Folk by denying either money or meeting rooms (usually schools) for local groups. The London Borough of Wandsworth was an example, despite the fact that an active Folk member, Bill Ballantine was a Labour councillor in the Borough. In 1978 a Tory governor of a school where a local group met, having read the *Leaders' Manual* complained of the Folk's 'political indoctrination' especially of older children who, he alleged, were required to become members of the co-operative movement. This, he said, placed the Folk on the same footing as the youth organisation of any political party and hence rendered them ineligible to use school premises. Despite the smear campaign, however, the Folk achieved a major breakthrough in 1976 when, under a Labour Government, the Department for Education and Science agreed for the first time to award it grant aid. Other voluntary youth organisations had been in receipt of this for many years. At last, the fact that the Woodcraft Folk had some friends among Labour MPs[19] paid off!

1980s

By the late 1970s it was clear that the Woodcraft Folk had arrived at a crossroads in its development. Membership continued to rise. In 1977 a Development Officer was appointed in the north of England (Doug Bourn) and in 1984 another was appointed to cover the south.[20] However, the Folk became, to some extent, a victim of its own success. Differences of opinion arose as to the future direction of what some saw as an embryonic mass youth movement. Margaret White reported a 'distressing feature' of the 1979 ADC was the existence of a '"we and they" situation'.[21] This was in evidence in other respects. The recommendations following 1981 Venturer camp were not confined to camping and attempted to address the divisive atmosphere. It was recognised in the first instance that the growth of the Folk meant that it could no longer be assumed that all areas would observe the same practices as was the custom when the organisation was small 'and the leadership more intimately known to each other'. Furthermore it acknowledged that a movement advocating social change 'must be careful to avoid insularity and observing tradition for tradition's sake' and that such traditions 'cannot be allowed to become a barrier to the acceptance of new ideas'. If the traditions or customs are useful then their purpose needs to be explained. However it was also recognised that members of long and outstanding service who are likely to have 'an emotional, vested interest in preserving the integrity of their past experience' do not want to see this undervalued or treated lightly. This plea for respect and toleration was easier to call for than to carry out. The columns of the new Folk magazine, *Focus*, reflected the 'old guard' vs 'young guard' debate. In a paper commissioned by the National Council of Voluntary Organisations in 1988 and written by a Woodcraft Folk leader[22] the problem in the Folk was described as being a clash between the old 'ritualistic culture' and the more modern values of new recruits, young parents who had not themselves come from Folk families but had been attracted to the organisation because it embodied principles they could identify with - equality, peace, international friendship, feminism and anti-racism. This, argued the author of the paper, contrasted sharply with the somewhat exclusive club which, it was alleged, the Folk had been up to the 1950s whereby unity had been achieved around a set of rituals (Woodcraft Folk weddings, christenings, naming ceremonies etc) which encouraged the notion that 'when you join the Folk you join for life'. The network of personal and family relationships which the 'ritualistic culture' of the Folk engendered and which formed the traditional base of the organisation, was, so the argument ran, no longer able to sustain a fast growing organisation. The author concluded that it was now impossible to reconcile the Folk's past with the kind of progressive future that a mass youth and children's organisation demanded. However it was also recognised that this new membership was predominantly middle class and thus steps would have to be taken to 'redress the balance'.[23] Jim Barr was the Woodcraft Folk Strathclyde Project Worker. He noted that although the Folk had developed over past five years (since 1980), most of this growth was in middle class or 'trendy' areas. This, he argued, was an inevitable consequence of appealing to peace and environmental groups given that such groups were unlikely to be found in working class areas. If the Folk was to grow in working class areas - a development which Barr strongly favoured - it had to recognise that in areas of high deprivation 'we are looking for people who aren't necessarily coming into the Folk with their first thoughts on the aims and principles'. He advocated a different approach of the type being used in Strathclyde where contacts were made with the community education service, tenants' associations, mother & toddler groups, summer play schemes as well as trade unions and trades councils.

Doug Bourn, the National Secretary appointed in 1984, clearly reflected the kind of 'young guard' type thinking expressed above. In 1989 he presented a report on the Folk's development and its future - *Part of the Mainstream of Society*. In introducing this he argued[24], on much the same lines as Barr, that although the Folk had grown in the 1980s 'a lot of the expansion has come from a relatively narrow social base, progressively minded parents who have been looking for some sort of alternative for their children'. However, he reported that the National Council had concerns about this. It its view the potential for the creation of a broad based movement was hampered by the inherent dangers of 'retreatism and exclusivity' brought about by the large number of parents who see the Folk as a 'haven from the worst excesses of society'. He continued:

> the Woodcraft Folk regarded itself as the progressive alternative and we saw the rise of new social movements as a natural support of our work. However, it has conjured up the image of the Folk as predominantly white and middle class. Support from minority communities remains minimal. Most groups in large towns and cities exist in the more prosperous areas. A high proportion of our leaders work in such professions

such as teaching, social services and local government.

According to Bourn, this was compounded by another problem which had emerged a decade before:

> The Woodcraft Folk in the '70s was seen by some of the press as a left wing children's movement. While the movement has clearly broadened its base, there are still dangers that some people could misconstrue our educational basis.

Thus in 1981 Doug Bourn had recommended that the *Pioneer Song Book* be carefully pruned of its overtly political songs (eg 'The Internationale' and 'Children of Workers') and songs from the then socialist countries of Eastern Europe (eg 'Song of the Komsomols'). Such songs, he said, had 'political connotations way outside the scope of the Folk'[25] and in addition (according to HMIs Bourne had spoken to) created political problems for the Folk.

Clearly then left wing politics which had, in one form or another, served the Folk in good stead since its inception, was now regarded as the incorrect identity for the Folk. Bourn also explicitly rejected the all too prevalent view of the Woodcraft Folk 'some form of alternative to the Scouts and Guides'. Instead, the Woodcraft Folk was to see itself 'as providing a range of activities for children and young people, giving them a choice alongside other organisations such as the Scouts and Guides'. Hence according to this view, the Folk was an integral part of the youth service - a view which was predicated upon an Albermarle-type vision of a well funded statutory and voluntary youth service. However, the problem was that the kind of funding needed was so much reduced at national and local level, that it rendered the hopes for the youth service and the Folk's place within it somewhat fanciful.

Although the Woodcraft Folk's participation in the Youth Service was of great benefit financially until the late 1980s, it was also fraught with the danger of incorporation. The question is, in the long term, did the accommodation the Folk had to make in order to comply with the rules governing funding, reduce its distinctive identity? The very title of the 1989 report, *Part of the Mainstream of Society* is indicative of such a process. Certainly compared to the 1930s the Folk in the 1980s would have been unrecognisable. This not just because so many of the Folk traditions had gone, but because, as we have seen, the Folk was nowhere near as overtly political as it was then. In the 1930s it was an unmistakably socialist and class conscious organisation which saw its prime aim as educating children and young people in a variety of novel ways, for the purpose of achieving social change. The child-centred educational methods it used were ahead of their time, but mainstream education, albeit for different purposes, began to catch up with the Folk's pedagogical approach by the 1970s hence lessening the distictiveness of the Folk's appeal in this respect too. It is clear that the political aspect of the Folk's work had already begun to change after the second world war. It would be incorrect to suppose that all the most radical changes were initiated in the 1980s. To suppose that all the most radical changes were brought about by the newer members recruited in the 1970s and 1980s is something of a simplification. Certainly they regarded themselves as the harbingers of change, fighting fossilised, ritual ridden oldies, but as Margaret White put it in 1979:

> I cannot accept from our younger critics that the movement, particularly the older members are loathe to accept change. Progress made including tremendous changes in the application of our work had been outstanding in the post-war period. Some of you would never believe how long it took the movement to change from wearing jerkins to shirts; to revise National Council structure; to use first names instead of Folk names ... Maybe some of our current leaders, especially those new to the Woodcraft Folk could never envisage the Folk's contribution to CND marches ... it's unfair to suggest that new ideas are not considered and applied on their merit.[26]

Nonetheless the Folk was late, compared to other labour movement organisations in understanding and tackling racism and sexism. The debate on these issues was begun in a modest way in the columns of *Focus* in 1982/3 and it is clear from the correspondence columns and from the limited amount that can be gleaned from ADC reports that there was great opposition not just from older members, but from those who thought that such issues were middle class fads. In this respect the debate in the Folk mirrored that of almost all predominantly white labour movement organisations. Apart from the fact that the Folk's debate was so much later and that it appeared not to have noticed what had been going on elsewhere, the only other surprise was the fact that on the issue of sexism the Folk was not much more advanced given that it had always (unlike the rest of the labour movement) had women leaders, and because of its commitment to sex equality, had pioneered co-educational youth work.

On the issue of racism, even the cautious British Youth Council was more advanced than the Folk. In 1984 it had moved beyond the discussion stage - the stage Woodcraft Folk had just begun - and had published its 'anti-racialist' education pack. Today Woodcraft Folk is fully committed to, and actively promotes, equality of opportunity and thus understands the need to tackle racism, sexism and homophobia - but this has taken a long time and it may be that the identity of the Folk has been negatively affected by the delay.

Notes

1   *Memorandum on the Reconstruction of the Folk to Meet Post-War Conditions*, YMA/WF/13
2   National Folk Council Memorandum to all-Councils' meeting 7-8th December 1946, YMA/WF/26
3   S Poole, 'Cogitations of an Old Codger: the Folk Trail Then and Now', *Focus*, Autumn 1986
4   Annual Report 1962 - WF archive
5   This was one of a regular series of courses/seminars for youth leaders of affiliates of the International Falcon Movement.
6   Presumably Rawson took this from Engels' *Origin of the Family, Private Property and the State*
7   Report of IFM Helper Course 1964 *International Camp Work*, YMA/WF/166
8   Jess Cawley 'Camping the Woodcraft Way', *Focus* no.7, June 1983
9   *National Council Statement on Venturer Camp 1989* WF archive
10   General Secretary's Report to National Council, 4th February 1978 (M White), WF archive
11   General Secretary's Report to National Council, 3rd October 1981 (M White), WF archive
12   National Secretary's Report to National Council, June 1985 (D Bourne), WF archive
13   General Secretary's Report to National Council, 4th February 1978 (M White), WF archive
14   B Davies *Threatening Youth*, Open University Press p98
15   *Youth and Community Work in the 1970s*, YSDC 1969 (quoted in B Osgerby *Youth in Britain since 1945*, Blackwell 1998
16   John Davis *Youth and the Condition of Britain*, Athlone Press 1990
17   Letter dater 23rd October 1975, signed O C D Mitchell, organisation and legal officer, WF archive
18   4th January 1976
19   Joan Lestor MP is an example. Both her children were members and she spoke publicly in favour of the Folk when it was under attack.
20   Rae Levy was the first person to occupy this post. Her employment was terminated shortly after Doug Bourn was appointed National Secretary. The reason for this remains shrouded in mystery and no documentary evidence remains, although many individuals have strong and conflicting opinions on the matter.
21   Secretary's report to National Council, April 1979 - WF archive

22 Elizabeth Crouch *National Bureaucracy & Local Anarchy- the Future of Democracy in the Folk*. The paper was delivered at an NCVO seminar for chief executives of voluntary organisations. Extracts of it were published in article published in *Focus*, Autumn/Winter 1987/8. The author was a Woodcraft leader in Kelvedon, Essex

23 Jim Barr, *Redressing the Balance - developing groups in working class areas*, Focus Autumn/Winter 1986/7.

24 1989 ADC Report

25 *Comments on proposed changes to song books*, D Bourn 23/9/81 - for National Council, 3rd October, WF archive

26 Secretary's report to National Council, April 1979 - WF archive

Chapter 9

EPILOGUE

What of the Woodcraft Folk today? A full answer would be inappropriate in a book attempting to analyse its past. All too rapidly the present becomes the past and the concerns of the early years of the 21st century will be overtaken by other events as yet unknown. Nonetheless, a few words on the continuities and the discontinuities of Woodcraft Folk might not be out of place.

The Woodcraft Folk is steeped in tradition and is proud of its past. It would appear, on the face of it, that the Folk's aims and activities, despite modification and revision, have changed little fundamentally over 75 years. Organisationally it is also very similar. It is still co-educational catering for Elfins (six to nine year olds), Pioneers (10-12), Venturers (13-15) and District Fellows (older self organised teenagers and young adults). The focus of its provision is more evenly spread among the age ranges than it was in the early years, although it is inevitably more difficult to retain older teenagers than younger children. Over 500 groups meet around the country, mainly in urban areas and Group activities are co-ordinated by adult volunteers, who hold regular informal meetings to plan the weekly programme of activities. Green shirts have given way to green T-shirts or sweat shirts, but the symbol and motto remain the same. Finance continues to be a problem. Children pay small weekly subscriptions, towards the cost of running group nights and trips away. In addition adult volunteer members and supporters pay an annual membership subscription. The national organisation receives a small grant from the Department for Education and Employment and also relies on donations from trade unions and other organisations sympathetic to the Folk's aims and objectives. However, as in the past the Woodcraft Folk relies overwhelmingly on the co-operative movement for financial and material support. Outdoor activities, especially camping, are still an important feature of Woodcraft Folk activity. All districts have an annual camping programme and every 4-5 years an international camp is held. In addition regular use is made of the Folk's outdoor centres. These have expanded in recent years - the two earliest, Lockerbrook (in the Peak district) and Cudham (North Downs), established in 1964 and 1974 respectively, have been supplemented by Hamsterley Forest (North Pennines), the County Centre (Suffolk) and Height gate (South

Pennines). In addition Woodcraft have three campsites.

The aims and values of Woodcraft in the 21st century demonstrate a strong continuity with the past. Current publicity material describes the Folk thus:

> It's co-operative. We encourage children and young people to work together to share their skills and enthusiasm. It believes in equal opportunities and access for all its members. This means being able to discuss and challenge discrimination. It is open to people of any religion or none. It aims to empower young people to make decisions themselves and to take an active part in the world about them. It is dedicated to the building of a more peaceful future. It promotes an understanding of the need to protect our environment and the use of the world's resources. It has exchanges with similar organisations throughout the world. Our international links help to further our motto: Span the World with Friendship.

However, as this book has shown, despite many continuities, much has changed. Indeed the organisation would not have survived had it not been able to adapt itself, for better or worse, to the spirit of the age. Thus it is that the search for focus and identity still continues. This task would appear to be more difficult in the 21st century since in many respects the Woodcraft Folk has been the victim of its own success. Many of the child-centred educational methods it pioneered have now become embedded within official state pedagogic practice. Its commitment to equality, ecology, peace and other progressive issues, no longer identifies the Folk as special since the issues themselves are no longer marginal - they have entered into mainstream discourse and, to some extent, the practice of a large section of society. This is not to lay any false claims that the Folk alone was responsible for such developments, but rather to note that the climate in which it is operating has changed significantly since the early days. Thus it was that in 1998 the Folk launched a new strategic plan, *Dancing to a Stronger Beat*. The Woodcraft Folk hailed the launch of this plan as one of the most important initiatives in its recent history. The five strategic objectives which it addresses are certainly not new: Raise the profile; Strengthen the movement; Improve our educational work; Make the most of our resources; Find the finance. It remains to be seen whether, if implemented, the desired results will be forthcoming.

In 1975 Leslie Paul declared that he was surprised that the Folk was still in existence. In an interview with John Hodgson, the full text of

118

which is reprinted below, Paul was asked whether there was still a role
for the organisation he founded.

John Hodgson: Is there a role for movements like the Woodcraft Folk
today?

Leslie Paul: I would have said, you see, until a couple of years ago that
the Woodcraft Folk was a dead duck. I would have said it had
run out of steam and was still living on the ideals and concepts
of the '20s and had very little to offer excepting to a few
people in society for whom it was a congenial way for leisure
activity. I rather changed my mind, I think in the last two
years. Something about the Woodcraft Folk in the last two or
three years impressed me very deeply. One has been its
capacity to withstand youth culture, not completely, but pretty
well - better than any other movement I can think of. But it
still retains its own integrity; its own culture which is not
created for it by the youth culture - which is largely an
American import. It has something native and indigenous
about it, and it's extraordinarily powerful. I find myself at a
loss to understand why it has produced such a binding loyalty -
but it does! And this is most impressive. So that it means
whatever one did when one built it, one did something very
strong; one created a bond that was very strong. Now I think
with the growth of the ecological movement - the
environmental movement, a sense of ... not so much back to
nature, as back to the locality. What happens in the locality is
very important culturally; much more important than we ever
thought it was in the '20s - though we were doing it! We now
see this as an important social movement. So I would say that
any movement, irrespective of whether it is the Woodcraft folk
or not, which can produce active, self governing, autonomous
groups in the locality doing their own thing is terribly
important socially. And it may never be; I don't think it will
ever be a great movement in numbers - if it ever got up to
50,000 I should be surprised. But, you see, I now see
something else which, a long life of history has taught me, that
size may be the enemy of the value of a movement rather than
a signal of it. I would think the Scouts were more important
when they were 10,000 strong or 20,000 strong before 1914,
than they were in the '30s when they were a million strong or
something. They were more important in their social impact,

119

and I think the Folk could remain important in its social impact. I was also impressed, and I am still impressed, by the fact that when the lefties, whether Trotskyists or Communists or whatever come into the Woodcraft Folk, what they seem to become is Woodcraft Folk. Not sort of infiltrators and propagandists, but that falls behind them.

Thus for Paul the key to the survival of the Folk lay in its 'otherness', its capacity to close ranks against the dominant culture thereby creating an alternative counter cultural group loyalty. He recognised that such a perspective would preclude the possibility of the Folk becoming a mass youth organisation, but for him this was no bad thing. However, this is precisely why many were critical of the Woodcraft Folk in the 1970s and argued that it had to become part of the mainstream if it was to grow. It is the dilemma faced by its leaders today. What image must the Folk project if it is to grow? Does being 'part of the mainstream' necessarily entail rejecting the values of the past? So far I have mentioned only the continuities, but what of the discontinuities? The most important of these is the political orientation of the Folk - its socialist perspective - which in turn was responsible for its attraction to working class activists. For reasons which have been explained, the most overtly political phase in the Folk's history in the 1930s, was more muted after the war. It was still there as could be seen in its brave stance against the cold war. But it was more muted still from the 1970s onwards partly through fear of losing state funding and partly because socialist politics did not fit the more mainstream agenda advocated at the time. Clearly one cannot transpose the political climate of the 1930s into this decade, but on the other hand it would be a mistake to suppose that commitment is unknown amongst the young, or indeed their parents. Whilst the Woodcraft Folk never made the mistake of becoming an adjunct of any other organisation or political party, its broad-brush non-aligned socialism was expressed through its class conscious ideological standpoint and it was this which earned it life-long loyalty from the many workers and their families drawn to its ranks. It was this loyalty which helped sustain the organisation through its many vicissitudes. However, some members in the 1970s argued that it was precisely this kind of 'in-group' loyalty that prevented the growth of the Folk. There can be no doubt that the Folk's membership grew rapidly in the 1970s, but there is not necessarily a causal connection between this fact and the jettisoning of some of the political values of the past. On the other hand, it is clearly the case that merely proclaiming the socialist credo would not result in a flood of class conscious parents volunteering themselves and their offspring to the Woodcraft Folk cause. However this does not mean that such an ideology is inherently unattractive and must perforce be consigned forever to the dustbin of history. Perhaps the real challenge is to be able to distinguish between the core principles underlying an organisation and the more ephemeral aims and objects. Aims and objects need constant re-working and revision; core principles are not biblical tenets, they too must be presented in a way which can appeal to each generation, but in a manner which preserves their essence.

There is no magic formula which unlocks the secret of the appeal to youth. The scout and guide movements are not the mass organisations they once were. The countervailing attractions of the music, club and drug scene are such powerful rivals that it is a wonder that non-commercial youth work still exists. Leslie Paul was probably correct in assuming that the Folk would never be a mass youth organisation. The question is should it aspire to be and if it does will it lose the core principles which have guaranteed its survival, against all the odds, for the past 75 years. History will be the judge.

APPENDIX I

WOODCRAFT FOLK MEMBERSHIP FIGURES 1925-1983

Compiled from Annual Reports and IFM returns. After 1983 individual membership, other than Adult membership, was not recorded. A system of Group Registration was introduced which while giving a more accurate picture of Woodcraft Folk activity, was far less accurate in respect of individual, non-adult membership. This system is still used. It is only possible to guess at the total membership by guessing that size of each group averages at around 15-20 children or young people.

1925	70
1928	c500
1930	c980
1931	
1932	
1933	1,076
1934	1,432
1935	2,191
1936	3,260
1937	3,518
1938	4,321
1939	5,134
1940	2,558
1946	2,892
1947	3,286
1952	3,900
1953	4,000
1962	6,500
1973	11,355
1974	12,862
1975	14,780
1976	14,173
1977	14,618
1978	14,663
1979	14,724
1980	15,145
1981	14,864
1982	15,125
1983	15,966

Appendix II

ORAL HISTORY

The following pages are transcriptions of interviews taken from the Oral History Archive of the Woodcraft Folk. This project was started by Paul Bemrose who has conducted two of the interviews reprinted here. The third, with Leslie Paul, is part of a longer interview of him conducted by John Springhall. John kindly donated his tapes to the Woodcraft Folk. I wish to record my thanks to Paul Bemrose both for transcribing the interviews and for permission to use this material.

LESLIE PAUL:
Interview with John Springhall 7 August 1976

Can you say something about Stanley Hall's recapitulation theory?
Yes. I discussed this with my friend Osbert Walter while I was still at school and he had already left it. Before I was 16 I had read McDougall's *Psychology* in the Open University Library and another book, I think I may still have it, called by a Catholic priest, a man called F A Servante on the psychology of the boy. Because then I was a patrol leader in the Scouts and was supposed to know something about the kids I was looking after. It will have been mentioned somewhere at that time Stanley Hall's *Adolescence* and I think Osbert Walter picked it up and either showed it to me or lent it to me or we got it out of the library - somehow or other it got into my hands. I must confess as a schoolboy I found it absolutely beyond me. But the general idea, just then I was accepting evolutionary philosophy, was easy to assimilate. But of course it became quite rapidly the most cranky educational idea ever invented. Osbert Walter, who started his own group quite outside my own movement at Browning Settlement in Walworth Road for a couple of years and then abandoned it. He wrote an educational programme based entirely upon the recapitulation theory, which ended up with the proposal that children should dig trenches, hide in the trenches, and throw stones at each other in order to assimilate the experience of the first world war. Now 1 0 Evans produced a similar programme, recapitulation programme, which had the same kind of idea, creating stages through which you pushed these kids. I think it still saturates the ideas of *Child & the Race*. I think it's a little more vaguely there in *The Folk Trail*, its gone by the time we produced *The Training of Pioneers*. And then in *The Republic of Children* I criticise the theory and abandon it.

What about Ernest Thompson Seton. Was he a great influence on you?
Yes. Before I left school I absorbed *The Book of Woodcraft*, if its possible to absorb that crazy book. But I looked at all the illustrations and read all the bits that interested me anyway. And it wasn't so much what was actually said in the book, it was the whole atmosphere it created which rushed out of the pages at you. Osbert Walter who was my kind of running mate in these early years, he bought it and he'd only just left school so it was in his library and I could borrow it whenever I wanted and looked it through and then we both began to read ETS nature Stories, his *Two Little Savages* and his whole host of nature stories. So in two or three ways from the age of 14 or 15 he was a great

influence on me. But what most excited Osbert Walter and I was the treatment of the American Indian. We became defenders of the American Indians in our minds and in our talks with one another and in our talk with other people. This genocide of the American Indians-which is mostly in the last chapter of *The Book of Woodcraft* and it was this in a way more than his American Indianism which excited us. It was our first bit of political education.

What impression at that age did John Hargrave have upon you?
Well again of course, hero-worship impression. He was a very assured man, aggressive; an interesting man you see. He fought in Gallipoli, had all this scouting experience, then having the audacity to challenge and criticise Baden-Powell and come out because after all Baden Powell had been one of our boyhood heroes. So we were fascinated by him, absolutely fascinated by him. He had a charisma. I remember visiting his place, Wayside at Kings Langley, shows how much he impressed me that even the address comes back so easily. The place was full of his paintings, he'd even done murals across the walls of his bungalow, which I suppose wasn't even as big as this one, but it certainly impressed us. I remember one painting that he had of primitive man, Neanderthal man or something like that going across a plain, hardly call it a desert naked, and the rain was falling. The title of picture was "Hell", the endless rain was falling on this little group of nomads.

Well, of course, all that kind of thing was deeply impressive to youngsters coming out of what was it - lower middle class environment in the suburbs - in which there wasn't a great deal of intellectual excitement or even much challenge. The Scouts had been the greatest challenge in one's childhood.

Was it at this time you started to move towards socialism through people you met through Kibbo Kift?
Yes - not initially. Kibbo Kift did not strike us, Walter and I, as a socialist movement. What it struck us as being was an elite which had separated itself from the world, we talked scathingly about the "masses" - of the great unwashed and all this kind of thing. A fine sense of superiority ... of feeling that we were apart from this wretched humanity! I mean that Ankh Lodge "seven erudite" you see is elitism - its school boy elitism - its very, very, interesting. So we didn't feel that. But then of course my career was different from Peakes. I started a Lodge; which was Men of Endeavour shortened which met in the spare room of my parents' house. From this I got elected to the Headmanship

of Brockleything - I was only 17. It was the last thing I expected. Lord Wilmot was there, very irate with me because after being elected I was expected to make a speech. I didn't know what to say. I was too green. He said 'Get on with it! Get on with it!' I can still remember him saying that. I didn't know what I was supposed to get on with, I was only a boy you know. Brockleything was a co-operative and labour enterprise. Wilmot was already candidate of East Lewisham Labour Party. And Ellis of course was a socialist and an agent for Ramsay MacDonald in the famous 1918 election.

What distinguished the ideas behind the Woodcraft Folk and Kibbo Kift?
At first very little. When this quarrel about my Headmanship, it didn't dawn upon me at that moment that this was anything to do with politics, it only seemed to me someone trying to work the book - the regulations. It only dawned on me as the quarrel developed that it was also a political issue. It wasn't debated as a socialist issue, it was debated as a democratic issue. So we were doing a Hobbes and Locke job, we were arguing in our group what were democratic principles and how they should be applied in this movement called Kibbo Kift. It became more and more obvious as we went on with this argument that Kibbo Kift was a one man show. Hargrave made all the decisions and carried all the power. However, autonomous the local groups might be, as far as the national movement was concerned we had no power. Hargrave had it all. And moreover what we didn't like was the existence of this rather shadowy Lodge around him of sort of manipulators. A number of people around him seemed to be manipulating the movement as his rather shadowy - well not bodyguard even but more as his Gestapo. We never thought of that in those days, but we didn't like power in the hands of people who weren't ever accountable. The Folk tried to get away - well did get away from this structure right away in that as soon as we were established by a meeting of all the adult leaders of all the groups who proceeded to elect the various officers, so that at the very beginning we had an assembly and elected officers. And these officers were elected, as far as I can remember at the annual meeting, year after year. They weren't there in perpetuity.

Was there any element of anti-capitalist, anti-urban industrial opposition in the Woodcraft movements?
Yes. This was very powerful. You see when I spoke about the genocide of the Indians which Seton reported in the *Book of Woodcraft*, this was almost our first initiation into any - industrialism, and imperialism - the

way the west was going. As school boys we were outraged by the thought that these developing western nations had simply massacred these primitive people who were so much admired. Don't forget that any schoolboy of any merit then had read Fennimore Cooper and idealised the Indians before we knew Ernest Thompson Seton. He only gave us, as it were, the facts that supported our view of the American Indians.

You see the other side of it, apart altogether from the American Indians was William Morris - *News from Nowhere* and *The Dream of John Bull*. Morris' writings fitted in toward democracy better than either of those books fitted in with Ernest Thompson Seton. We had a view of a sort of medieval England. After all one of the attractive things about Kibbo Kift was the wearing of this cowl, you see that gave over the medieval appearance to you immediately. And so there was a stream of a pre industrial England, even I suppose the term "Woodcraft Folk" comes from this conception.

Prynn brings out rather interestingly, a kind of conflict in the Woodcraft Folk between building a new society on socialist lines and escaping from the existing society into camping and woodcraft. He sees this as a contradiction or even a weakness in the Woodcraft Folk. But it was a strength, because you see nearly all great movements have some kind of ambiguity about them. Boy Scouts had it in exactly the same way. Were you defending your country, or were you becoming a jolly good, noble chap in your local society - doing your good turn every day. They all have contradictions like this. I think we were trying to satisfy two impulses at one and the same time was quite good because the two impulses were there to be satisfied. So I don't regard this as a weakness. Its true we didn't see it very clearly; but we did see it clearly after a time and did talk about this contradiction.

BASIL RAWSON:
Interview with Peter Gilpin (undated)

How did the Woodcraft Folk come to your attention? How did you get involved?

Well the involvement in the Folk arose really out of a sense of disillusionment as well as disappointment in the effect of propaganda. I was 29 when after these years of work with the ILP - successful work in many ways, because we did have a big impact. We won many converts, not just to the Labour Party but to socialist thinking because the ILP stressed not the material advantages of socialism as the social need for socialism, the attitudes to each other and so in other words there was a strong idealism running through ILP propaganda. I'd had the experience of being howled down in the poorest quarters of Sheffield, in speaking about nursery schools for instance

I was protagonist of nursery schools because I realised its advantage in what to me then was socialist education, preparation of children to be better, not only physically but mentally and socially. So I looked upon the nursery school as a progressive kind of school which would lead to a better development of the child. I was one of the main propagandists in Sheffield and it fell to my lot at an ILP conference in 1927, I think it was, to move a resolution by Sheffield ILP that committed the ILP to this cause amongst others. And in propaganda for it, which was usually street corner propaganda, we only used school halls at election time, it was there amongst the poorest section in one of the slum districts in Sheffield that I could see this terrible lack of understanding of what was necessary, which led to opposition. And that and other experiences also led me to feel that something more was needed for socialist advance than mere propaganda to the adults. I'd long been conscious of the way that adults are victims of the society in which they grow up and you needed more than propaganda to help them change their minds. They'd change their minds if they got a kick in the pants in the sole materialist considerations, which often entered into winning Labour votes, which to my mind was never sufficient. I could see a danger in winning votes for socialism just through material considerations as the bait. So that obviously, even in that time, I was interested already in what was more than propaganda - it was socialist education.

No doubt a lot of my speeches were educational rather than propagandist, which led to their effect being probably more permanent in many minds. At least that was the results that seemed to be apparent. And it was in 1928 that I came to the conclusion that the key to socialist education was in the work on minds that would be more receptive to change in attitudes and ideas. In other words it was through education of children - socialist education of children - that one would stand a better chance of getting the right sort of individual who would make the biggest contribution to changing society in the right direction.

I was already playing with the idea of organising a little independent group. In 1926 I started to organise a rambling club for Brightside section of the ILP. Brightside ILP was good ground on which to start the attention which I felt was necessary to the regenerative factors of outdoor activities. There was also the rebel side of rambling in those days because rambling organisations were getting together to fight for access to the countryside. Particularly moorlands and the mountains, on which we were forbidden to walk because of the necessity, so called, of keeping the moors for a few days grouse shooting every year. The ILP rambling club also took on the old task of the Clarion ramblers, and they included socialist propaganda in our work. That is we set up a meeting place in many villages on route, on Sundays sometimes in a quiet place wed have discussions of our own on the problems of socialism and the way to it. So even the rambling club became a good propaganda force. It was a family club, insofar as members brought their children with them. So there was always a group of children there. And of course my old attachment to young people meant that I had considerable influence with the youngsters. I could often help them and in fact many of them began to bring their problems to me which it appears they hadn't raised with their parents. And it did impress me with the fact that even in socialist homes, children did need something. I was convinced by the end of the rambling season - well it never ended for us insofar as the families were concerned but children began to drop off in winter.

And it was in December, or November - I forget which month - in 1928 when there was an article that appeared in the *New Leader* that was the ILP magazine - 'Why Not a Labour Scout Movement?' written by Leslie Paul. Well whilst I had already met Fenner Brockway who already had his connection with the Folk, there hadn't been any mention of the Folk up to that time And that article immediately gave me a clue as to connect in some way. If this movement was engaged in socialist education - if it wasn't just another copy of the scout movement - then there would be something in it. So I wrote off to London. I got a letter from the secretary. I don't know his ordinary name; it was Osio the scribe, because at that time they used Woodcraft names entirely, even officially. He sent me a copy of *Wide Awake*, newly printed at that time, and gave me a modicum of information, which convinced me this was something worthwhile. So I wrote off to Leslie Paul with a series of questions and the answer to those questions satisfied me insofar as I could see the elements of socialist education, the practice of democracy, co-education - which was one of the high points of the nursery school of course - and those very things which I felt were essentials. I had my doubts about the mysticism of the Folk. I thought it might be escapist - I'd heard of the Wandervogel and I'd seen in the Wandervogel some faults. Not chauvinistic so much as escapist. However, I decided to have a talk about this organisation to the children of the rambling group. We were on a ramble in February and during the lunch time - I'd told the parents at a previous committee meeting what I'd heard about the Folk. They thought it would be a good idea, some of them didn't like the idea of the children separating from them. They liked the family grouping we'd got. But they could see the point that the children of ILP members could form a nucleus group and that by attracting children from outside - from the labour movement, the co-operative movement or even from outside we could begin a new thing in socialist education as distinct from socialist propaganda.

And at this meeting these youngsters - 11 of them, I explained what I knew about the Folk and I said the best thing we can do is not just to try and confine it to this particular meeting but let's have a ramble together. The opportunity came for a ramble on the second Sunday in April 1929. By that time I had also been selected as Labour candidate for a Conservative held division in Sheffield - Hallam division. It was the ILP's custom to fight propaganda fights in the Tory divisions and wards. I'd already been a candidate in Tory wards, not winning which would have caused complications, because I had my doubts about being in any kind of cage - whether it was the Council or Parliament. That's just a personal view. But we went on this ramble to one of the wildest areas near Sheffield - Stenage. There was a big, grit stone escarpment and there by a flat rock on which we sat we discussed this organisation. And the decision was taken, not by a majority but unanimously, that they would form a Woodcraft group. They first said they'd call it the ILP Woodcraft group, as it was formed from ILP children. But I suggested that the custom in the Folk seemed to be for groups to have a name and also we as individuals should also have names. Well this was a new idea. There was romanticism in it and the children had much more readiness for this than adults would have. One of the boys said "Well this is something new. In Indian or backwoodsman language were going to break a new trail. So shall we call ourselves the Trailbreakers?" And that became the name of

Sheffield's first group. I sent in requests for charters and signed up the group, and we started meeting in each others' homes for a time. Regularly meeting at weekends and in fact most of our business was done at weekends. We took our tents at weekends, we took Primus stoves and cooked our own meals cause you couldn't make fires everywhere, and we made our arrangements. It was realised that we would have to grow, we'd have to a meeting place.

HENRY FAIR:
Interview with Paul Bemrose 1988

How did you get involved in the Woodcraft Folk?
In 1926 as you know there was a General Strike. I had worked since I was 14 years of age. I established a youth section of the Labour Party before the days of the Labour League of Youth. My father was an active Trade Unionist and socialist and ergo being his youngster our room was the committee room, so we had people like Tania Shane, Ramsay MacDonald, and Jimmy Thomas come round. And I would help at election times. Anyway, I started up the youth section in 1921 and it was opposed by the head office of the Labour Party saying the time wasn't opportune to set up a youth movement. But we went ahead and I set up a group at Mitcham. Then I established a group in Kingston, another one at Wimbledon, another one at Worster Park and we built up a Surrey federation of unofficial youth sections. When Eccleston Square at the time said 'Well I think we ought to form a Labour League of Youth' and once it was established our adult party said 'Now Henry. Your groups have got to go into the League of Youth.' Well that's how I started.

Then in 1926, when I was 19, there was a General Strike and I thought that the revolution had arrived. On the 9th day of the General Strike we were stronger than we were on the first one. There wasn't a wheel turning without the permission of the TUC. There wasn't a lorry entering South London bus garage unless it had a TUC permit, and the police stood by and did nothing - couldn't do anything because we were in the majority. And then that night on the 9th day we heard on the radio that Jimmy Thomas and Ramsay MacDonald had sold the miners down the river. They had called off the General Strike.

What did you think about that?
I was appalled. I'm a pacifist, but.

Why didn't you leave the Labour Party then?
Well I did indirectly. In so far as all my spare time had been devoted to the Labour Party. I decided my problem, my job, my task, my objective now must be to train future leaders so they wouldn't do the same things as Jimmy Thomas and Ramsay MacDonald or anyone of that ilk.

Did you know Leslie Paul well?
Well yes. He was Headman of the Folk from the time I joined till 1933, when he stood down and Basil Rawson became Headman.

Why did he stand down?
I think he wanted to devote more time to writing and also he was undergoing certain fundamental changes himself. He was tending to become a little more religious. Of course as you know he finished up wholly employed at St Peters and St Paul's church in Cheltenham.

What do you think made Leslie Paul become religious?
I think he always did have it in him. If you look at some of his poetry and the words of some of the songs, there's a certain spiritual element I think he felt the need to worship something or to look upon something like that and he chose nature, plus the social content and so on. But later on in life I think the spiritual side got channelled in much more.

Leslie Paul came from what we'd say today was a middle class structure, his father had a good job in the print and Leslie had a good education, and his brother Kenneth got a job in a bank. He was the first person I knew who arrived on a campsite in a mechanical vehicle - a motorbike and sidecar.

Did you like Leslie Paul?
Yes I liked him in so many ways, although I used to pull his leg on a number of occasions! I was always in the working class and I used to pull his leg sometimes. For example, if I could illustrate it, we'd go into a café and I'd say, 'Have a cup of tea Leslie?' 'Yea.' 'Two teas please.' And Leslie would turn around and say, 'Would you make it China tea please?' And I used to feel so embarrassed.

Was he an intellectual?
He was a bit of an intellectual. If I can illustrate again. We went along to one Easter convention - Co-op gathering of educators to agitate for a bigger grant. I went along to support him and two or three others went up. But we all wore Woodcraft jerkins, shorts and things at the meeting. But Leslie, who didn't camp out with us, but slept in a bed and breakfast place, turned up in civvies. So Leslie got up to make a speech and the Chairman said 'Ah! Good morning Mr Paul. Where is your shirt this morning?' And he ribbed Leslie up hill and down dale. 'I see you haven't got your green shirt on this morning. Perhaps you haven't got enough shirts to go round.' The whole audience was roaring with laughter. Leslie Paul was standing up there looking very deflated and so on, and Leslie Paul said 'Mr Chairman. I haven't got my shirt on this morning. My shirt is on this resolution.' Everybody clapped him and he got an increase in our grant of about £10 per year.

Another thing about Leslie, at the 1937 camp in Brighton Leslie was going to camp down there for a period! 'But would you get me a bell tent Henry because I want to have a camp bed in it.' While the rest of us were sleeping on the floor. 'Henry do you think you could get someone who's prepared to run for me? You can't expect me to run all over the camp.' So he had a little fag as it were! I think he was a bit sceptical about having to descend, for want of a better term, to the levels of the ordinary working class person. When war broke out we were all subject to conscription. Leslie at that time was doing civilian work lecturing for the army but he was working down in Kent somewhere and the commanding officer said to him 'What's your future Mr Paul about the call up?' 'Oh!' he says, 'I come in the next age for calling up.' So the Captain is alleged to have said to him 'Well when you are called up quote my name and ask to be posted to the Army Educational Corp. Then you can come down here and carry on the work you're doing now.' And he wrote to me! it's a pity you don't keep these letters isn't it? - Saying of his changed situation, 'How pleased I am. I have my own room to sleep in and I'm not herded into a dormitory with the rest of them.'

Do you think Leslie Paul was disappointed with the Woodcraft Folk?
He was very critical when it started to develop a left wing political attitude. Let us say that the situation which was inherent at the beginning of the war when the Communist Party was opposed to taking part in the war because Russia wasn't involved. But immediately Russia was attacked by Germany the Communist policy completely reversed and they said you should all join the forces to protect the Soviet Union. And there were elements within the Folk who went with that you see, and he said he couldn't accept it you see.

What role did communists have in the early movement?
We always had them in the early movement because we had some very active, strong groups in east London who were up against the British Union of Fascists daily activities - so you could understand them. There was a demand at one time by the Hackney group for example who moved a resolution at ADC that amendment to Woodcraft Folk costume should include a red neckerchief!

We were brought up as leaders to thoroughly understand the history of the red Indian; because the Indian tribal system was as near to communism as would make no odds. And if we could get the principles of the Indian tribal system implemented in the movement we should be almost a perfect society.

What about the International camp in 1937 in Brighton?
It was manned completely by voluntary labour, the Brighton Society (Co-op) helped us a lot. We built a tower - Dick Penifold - he was a carpenter and a member of the Communist Party, but a very sincere co-operator. And he made it so that one side opened so you could get in and he made a ladder- so I could climb up the top and harangue the multitude!

What do you think of the modern Folk?
Well I've only flirted with them! The conference (ADC) itself I was appalled to see on the agenda 'This conference approves the setting up of a working party to examine the restrictions upon Lesbians and Gay rights and that we offer them every assistance.' Now if this had got out into the Mail or the Express or the Sun, they would have gone to town and they would have crucified the movement. The same way they crucified Peter Tatchell when he stood in the Bermondsey bye-election and he admitted he was a believer in gay rights. Now I see in the last report that a working party has been sitting. If it comes up again on the ADC agenda and it gets publicised god help the movement! I'm not saying there's not a problem there. But it's a problem that should be dealt with by an adult organisation and has in fact had consideration inside the Labour Party. It is not a problem that should be dealt with by an organisation that professes itself to be a children's movement.

BIBLIOGRAPHY

1 Primary sources

(i) archive

British Library of Economic and Political Science: The Youth Movement Archive (YMA)
- Archive of Kibbo Kith Kin
- Archive of the Woodcraft Folk (incomplete: much material at Woodcraft Folk House)

Public Record Office
- MEPO
- M15 papers KV 4/3, 4/54, 4/57

National Co-operative Archive
- Minutes of Co-operative Congresses
- Minutes of Co-operative Union Central Education Committee and Education Executive
- Co-operative Youth Collection

National Museum of Labour History
- Young Communist League Archive
- Communist Party Archive (Youth Affairs Advisory)

(ii) journals

a) Woodcraft
The Herald of the Folk
New Pioneer
The Pioneer
The Helper
Focus

b) International
Socialist Education International Bulletin
Falcons Outlook

c) Labour movement
Comrades
Labour Youth
Advance

(iii) published books and pamphlets

Economic League	Communism and British Youth, 1936
Forbush, W B	The Boy Problem, USA ,1907
Hall, G S	Adolescence, NY, 1920
Joad, C E M (Ed)	Manifesto: The Book of the Federation of Progressive Societies and Individuals, 1934
Paul, L	The Republic of Children, 1938
Paul, L	The Folk Trail, 1929
Paul, L	The Child and the Race
Paul, L	Angry Young Man, 1951
Paul, L	Early Days, 1980
Seton, E T	The Book of Woodcraft & Indian Lore, 1912
The League of Youth	Labour Party, 1931
Webb, S & B	Industrial Democracy, 1920
Wells, H.G.	A Short History of the World, 1929
Westlake, Aubrey	Woodcraft Chivalry, 1912

2 Secondary sources

(i) unpublished

Prynn, D	The Socialist Sunday Schools, the Woodcraft Folk and allied Movements (MA Thesis University of Sheffield), 1971

(ii) published books

Attfield, J	With Light of Knowledge - A Hundred Years of Education in the Royal Arsenal Co-operative Society, 1877-1977, 1981
Blanch, M	Imperialism, Nationalism & Organised Youth 1979
Davies, B	Threatening Youth, 1986
Davis, M	Comrade or Brother?, 1993

Davis, J   Youth & the Condition of Britain 1990

Eppe, H & Ullenberg   70 Years Socialist Youth International, Bonn 1977

Eppe, H & Lambert, O   The Falcon Organisations in East and Central
                            Europe from 1923 until now, nd

Evans, I O   Woodcraft & World Service, 1930

Fryer, P   Black People in the British Empire, 1993

Hendrick, H   Images of Youth: Age Class & the Male Youth
                            problem, 1990

MacDonald, R   Sons of the Empire, Toronto, 1993

Miliband, R   Parliamentary Socialism, 1961

Osgerby, B   Youth in Britain since 1945, 1998

Radomir, L   The History of the International Socialist
                            Youth Movement, Leyden, Sijthoff 1970

Rhodes, R   An Arsenal for Labour, 1998

Sirockin, P   The Story of Labour Youth, 1960

Solway, R   Demography and Degeneration, USA 1990

Springhall, J   Youth Empire & Society, 1997

Wagar, W W   H G Wells and the World State, Yale 1961

(iii) articles

Cooper, S   Pleasure, Politics and Co-operative Youth: the
                            interwar Co-operative Comrades' Circles,
                            Journal of Co-operative Studies, 32.2, September
                            1999

Finlay, J L   John Hargrave, the Green Shirts and Social
                            Credit, *Journal of Contemporary History*, vol.5
                            no.1 1970

Morris, B   Ernest Thompson Seton and the Origins of
                            Woodcraft Movements, *Journal of*
                            Contemporary History, vol.5, no.2, 1970

Wilkinson, P   English Youth Movements, *Journal of*
                            Contemporary History, vol.4, no.2, 1967

INDEX

heroic ideal, 22
hiking and camping, 20, 25, 32-33, 105-106, 117
Hocke, Willi, 86
Hungary, 89
Hurt, L A, 48, 49

imperialism, 11-17, 54-55
Interdepartmental Committee on Physical Deterioration, 15
International Co-operative Alliance, 50
International Falcon Movement (*see also* Red Falcon movement), 84-99
International Federation of Workers' Education Associations, 90
International Union of Youth and Students, 86-87

Joad, C E M, 62
Junior Circles, 46

Kempton, Fred, 51, 104
Kibbo Kift Kindred
 archive, 8-9
 development, 21, 22-23, 24-25
 hiking and camping, 25
 political philosophy, 23-25
 reasons for failure, 26-28
 segregation of sexes, 25
 split off of Woodcraft Folk, 26, 30-31
 uniform, 24, 26, 30
Kidd, Benjamin, 12-13
Knights of King Arthur, 22
Knorr, Lorenz, 88, 93

labour movement
 Labour Party development, 17
 Woodcraft Folk, 36, 54-66, 85
 youth organisations, 55-58, 59-61, 65-66
leaders, 16, 111-114
League of Youth, 55, 56-58

Mann, Tom, 73
Martinez, Miguel, 94, 97-98
Medasova, Zuzana, 76-77
Molnari, Sandor, 99
Morris, William, 34-35

National Co-operative Youth Organisation, 47-51
National Youth Conference Against War and Fascism, 72
No Conscription Fellowship, 69
No More War Movement, 69-70